Irish Women Writers: Texts and Contexts

Series editors: Kathryn Laing and Sinéad Mooney

Kathryn Laing (ed.), *Hannah Lynch's Irish Girl Rebels: 'A Girl Revolutionist' and 'Marjory Maurice'*
Elke d'Hoker (ed.), *Ethel Colburn Mayne: Selected Stories*
James H. Murphy (ed.), *Rosa Mulholland, Feminist, Victorian, Catholic and Patriot*

Advisory Board:
Heidi Hansson, Margaret Kelleher, Gerardine Meaney, James H. Murphy

Advance acclaim

This new edition of two of Hannah Lynch's stories amply realises the aims of the Irish Women Writers: Texts and Contexts series. Not only does it bring to the fore the work of a fascinating but often neglected writer, it is also brings two currently non-digitised periodicals into focus, one of which was edited by another neglected Irish woman writer. On two fronts, then, this work makes a significant contribution to our understanding of nineteenth-century writing by Irish women writers. Lynch's work is carefully contextualised by Kathryn Laing's rich and engaging introduction.

— **Beth Rodgers**, author of *Adolescent Girlhood and Literary Culture at the Fin de Siècle: Daughters of Today,* 2016.

Kathryn Laing's scrupulous scholarship provides a thoroughly realised and informative context for readings these long-out-of-print works by Hannah Lynch. *Marjory Maurice* and 'A Girl Revolutionist' demonstrate the uniquely multivalent quality of Lynch's fiction. Both texts adhere to conventional expectations of their genre without feeling stale or predictable, while at the same time, the works are slyly subversive, thanks to their Irish settings where characters argue questions of nation and identity, class and gender.

— **Maureen O'Connor**, author of *Edna O'Brien and the Art of Fiction,* 2021.

Hannah Lynch's Irish Girl Rebels:
'A Girl Revolutionary' and
'Marjory Maurice'

Irish Women Writers
Texts and Contexts

Hannah Lynch's
Irish Girl Rebels:
'A Girl Revolutionist' and 'Marjory Maurice'

Kathryn Laing

EER
Edward Everett Root, Publishers, Brighton, 2022.

EER
Edward Everett Root, Publishers, Co. Ltd.,
Atlas Chambers, 33 West Street, Brighton, Sussex, BN1 2RE, England.
Full details of our overseas agents in America, Australia, Canada, China, Europe, and Japan and how to order our books are given on our website.
www.eerpublishing.com

edwardeverettroot@yahoo.co.uk

We Stand With Ukraine!
EER books are **NOT** available for sale in Russia or Belarus.

© Kathryn Laing 2022.

Hannah Lynch's Irish Girl Rebels:
'A Girl Revolutionary' and 'Marjory Maurice'

ISBN: 9781913087319 Paperback
ISBN: 9781913087326 Hardback
ISBN: 9781913087333 Ebook

Irish Women Writers: Texts and Contexts Series, volume 1.

This edition © Edward Everett Root Publishers Co. Ltd., 2022.

Kathryn Laing has asserted her right to be identified as the owner of the copyright of this Work in accordance with the Copyright, Designs and Patents Act 1988 as the owner of this Work.

All rights reserved. No part of this publication may be reproduced, stored in a retrieval system or transmitted in any form or by any means, electronic, mechanical, photocopying, recording or otherwise, without the prior permission of the copyright owner.

Design and production by Pageset Ltd., High Wycombe, Buckinghamshire.

Contents

Acknowledgements ix

1. Timeline. 1

2. Introduction. 5
   Hannah Lynch: A Literary Life in Brief 5
   The Ladies' Land League, Land-War Fiction and Popular Print
   Culture 10
   The Irish New Woman and 'Marjory Maurice'. 15
   Girl's Realm: Publishing Contexts, the New Girl Fiction and 'A Girl
   Revolutionist' 20

3. A Note on the Texts 25

4. 'Marjory Maurice, a tale of our times', *Shamrock
   Magazine,* 27 December 1884–28 March 1885. 27

5. 'A Girl Revolutionist', *Girl's Realm,* vol. 1. no. 4, February
   1899. 185

6. Selected Bibliography. 197

The editor

KATHRYN LAING lectures in the Department of English Language and Literature, Mary Immaculate College, University of Limerick. With Dr Sinéad Mooney she is co-founder of the Irish Women's Writing Network (1880–1920) https://irishwomenswritingnetwork.com and also General Editor of the series, *Key Irish Women Writers* and *Irish Women Writers: Texts and Contexts* (EER Publishers).

Her research interests are principally in late nineteenth-century Irish women's writing, modernism and modernist women writers. She has published widely on Rebecca West, Virginia Woolf, George Moore and Hannah Lynch. Recent publications include *Irish Women Writers at the Turn of the Twentieth Century: Alternative Histories, New Narratives*, co-edited with Sinéad Mooney (Brighton: EER, 2020); *Hannah Lynch (1859–1904): Irish Writer, Cosmopolitan, New Woman* (Cork University Press, 2019), co-authored with Faith Binckes; "An Outpour of Ink": From the "Young Rebecca" to "The Most Important Signature of These Years": 1911–1920' in *Women, Periodicals, and Print Culture in Britain, 1890s–1920s: the Modernist Period*, eds. Faith Binckes and Carey Snyder (Edinburgh: Edinburgh University Press, 2019); K. Laing and Sowon Park, 'Writing and Politics: Writing the Vote: Suffrage, Gender, and Politics' in Vol 2 *Futility and Anarchy? British Literature in Transition 1920–1940*, eds. Charles Ferrall and Dougal McNeill (Cambridge: Cambridge University Press, 2018) and '"Only Connect": Irish Women's Voices, Latin America and the Irish Women's Writing Network', *Irish Migration Studies in Latin America* 9.1 (2018) http://www.irlandeses.org/wp-content/uploads/2018/01/women-6.pdf.

Acknowledgements

This volume was inspired by and grew out of a co-researched and co-authored project with Faith Binckes on the life and oeuvre of the late nineteenth-century Irish writer Hannah Lynch. This turned into our book, *Hannah Lynch 1859–1904: Irish writer, cosmopolitan, New Woman* (Cork University Press 2019), and with the riches of the material we discovered, and the fascinating details of Lynch's life and her contemporaries still coming to light, we knew there was more work to be done. This edition of two forgotten Ladies' Land League stories by Hannah Lynch, reproduced for the first time since their original publication, continues the process of recovery of the work of an extraordinary lost literary figure. Connecting with recent commemorations, it is also a tribute to the network and community of women who joined and were active in Anna Parnell's short-lived but pioneering feminist movement.

In addition to my ongoing discussions with Faith, I am indebted to a range of generous friends and colleagues for further conversations, for responses to my quirky queries in some cases (David Clare, Mary Pierse and Tadhg Foley in particular) and for detailed readings of the manuscript despite time pressures and constraints. To Sinéad Mooney, co-general editor of this important Texts and Contexts series, my thanks for editorial expertise, always incisive commentary and necessary good humour. Kristin Bluemel, serendipitous and ideal reader and commentator, offered a fresh and helpful perspective, noting the significance of the Ladies' Land League as a context for feminist community building, and feminist community as context for this particular critical intervention in feminist Irish literary studies. Caoilfhionn Ní Bheacháin's insights and shared knowledge in conversation were invaluable as the project developed. I am especially grateful to Beth Rodgers and Maureen O'Connor for their careful readings of the manuscript in its final stages, their astute critique, offering further insights and new material. I would like to thank Iliana Theodoropoulou for generously sharing the results of her intrepid archival research, helping me to confirm close connections between Olive Schreiner and Hannah Lynch and many more writers, besides. My thanks also go to Anne Nash who patiently transcribed both stories with such accuracy and speed.

For financial support towards research and transcribing the texts of both short stories I am indebted to the MIC Seed Funding Scheme.

Thanks are also due to John Spiers, Leigh Spiers and Nigel Austin at EER.

The text of the serialised novella, 'Marjory Maurice', published in *The Shamrock Magazine,* is reproduced courtesy of the National Library Ireland and the text of 'A Girl Revolutionist', published in *Girl's Realm,* is reproduced courtesy of the Bodleian Library, Oxford.

Timeline
Selected biographical, political, literary and publishing contexts[1]

1859 Hannah Lynch born on 25th March in **Dublin**.
1879 Founding of the Irish National Land League, 21 October, orchestrating the Land War and campaigning for land reform and tenants' rights in Ireland. Organised by Michael Davitt. Charles Stewart Parnell became president.
1881 31 January, **Dublin** – Ladies' Land League established by Anna Parnell at a meeting held at 39 Upper Sackville Street, Dublin.
21 February, **London**. Report of the inaugural meeting of London branch of the LLL, held 'yesterday afternoon' at Kenley Lodge, Macaulay Rd, Clapham, where Hannah Lynch was elected hon. sec.' (*The Freeman's Journal*, 22 February 1881).
13 August, **Dublin**. *United Ireland*, edited by William O'Brien (vol 1 no 1, 13 Aug 1881 – vol 17 no 888, 10 Sep 1898) is established. Originally the *Flag of Ireland*, an Irish Republican newspaper owned by Richard Pigott (vol 1 no 1, 05 Sep 1868 – vol 13 no 49, 06 Aug 1881), it was acquired by Parnell as a Land League paper.

---

1. This is an updated and abbreviated version of the timeline published in Binckes and Laing 2019, pp. 166–176.

12 October. Arrest of Parnell followed by arrests of other Land League members, including William O'Brien, the editor of *United Ireland*, and imprisonment in Kilmainham.

19 Oct-June 1881–82. 'La Puda de Monserrat'. Lynch's first publication (as far as is known) across two issues of the *Shamrock Magazine*.

15 December, **Dublin**. 'Lynch was present on 15 December for the most significant Dublin Metropolitan Police raid on the Abbey Street premises' of the Ladies' Land League' (Dungan 2014, p. 89).

16 December. Ladies' Land League declared an unlawful organisation; seizure of *United Ireland*.

Hannah Lynch and Rose Kavanagh take over editing proscribed *United Ireland*, and Lynch smuggles type out of Ireland according to various sources (Tynan 1913 and Henry George in Wenzer, ed. 2009).

1882 14 January, **Dublin**. Hannah and Nannie Lynch are arrested on 14 January 1882 (Schneller 2005, p. 201).

2 May. Kilmainham treaty and the release of political prisoners including Parnell, Dillon, and J. J. O'Kelly.

6 May – Release of Michael Davitt and the Phoenix Park Murders: assassination of Lord Frederick Cavendish, chief secretary and T.H. Burke, undersecretary.

8 August 1882 – Ladies' Land League dissolved.

1883 Olive Schreiner's *The Story of an African Farm* published, a novel identified as one of the first New Woman novels of the *fin-de-siècle* period.

1884–5 Lynch's 'Marjory Maurice' serialised in the *Shamrock Magazine*, 27 December 1884–28 March 1885.

1885 'Defeated'. London: *Beeton's Christmas Annual*. A land war and New Woman novel.

1891 *The Prince of the Glades*, 2 volumes, London: Methuen, 1891 (dedicated to Anna Parnell).

TIMELINE

1894 Sarah Grand's essay on the New Woman, 'The New Aspect of the Woman Question', published.
W.P. Ryan publishes *The Irish Literary Revival*.

1898 Launch of *Girl's Realm* in London with Alice Corkran as editor.

1899 *Autobiography of a Child*, Edinburgh and London: William Blackwood & Co. and New York: Dodd, Mead & Co, 1899. Lynch's most autobiographical novel, focused on a rebellious but suffering child, described at various points as the 'Dublin Angela', the 'English Angela', and the 'Irish rebel'.
'A Girl Revolutionist' published in *Girl's Realm*. vol. 1, no. 4, February 1899.

1900 'A Girl's Ride on an Engine', Lynch's second short story published in *Girl's Realm,* Vol. 2, March 1900.

1904 Died 9 January, Paris. Suffering from intermittent ill health all her life, Lynch died at the age of 44 after an operation to treat her stomach cancer.

Introduction

Hannah Lynch: A Literary Life in Brief

Hannah Lynch's novella, 'Marjory Maurice: a tale of our times' (1884–1885), and short story 'A Girl Revolutionist' (1899), bookend the final decades of the nineteenth century. Politically and culturally it was a period that was both turbulent and transformative in Ireland, marked by the violence of the land wars, the quest for Home Rule and the early stirrings of the Irish Literary Revival. Politically engaged and an aspiring writer from a young age, Dublin-born Lynch's writing offers a unique insight into this period. These stories, never reprinted and made accessible here for the first time, are based on her active involvement with the Ladies' Land League (1881–1882). This short-lived movement honed Lynch's political, feminist and literary affiliations already cultivated in a family that was, as her contemporary Katharine Tynan notes, 'all literary in so far as devotion to literature goes', and politicised: 'These sisters, with their mother, were quite at home amid the alarums and excursions of the Land League. ... These girls grew up among the writers, thinkers, orators, politicians, conspirators of their day' (1913, pp. 76–77). The nationalist affiliations and networks of both her mother, Anna (Calderwood) Cantwell, and step-father, James Cantwell, who had been a Young Irelander and associated with the Fenian movement,[1]

---

1. Lynch's father, Michael Lynch who died before she was born, also had nationalist associations and had been a successful merchant and shopkeeper in Dublin. For more biographical details about her mother and stepfather, see Binckes and Laing 2019, pp. 8–9.

nurtured this extraordinary environment, the couple presiding over a '*salon* in which nightly assembled a coterie of men and women who represented the talent and education of the Nationalists of Dublin' (Gibbs 1904, np).[2] In addition to these foundational influences, the Lynch-Cantwell sisters were well travelled from a young age, sent abroad either for schooling or in order to take up positions as governesses.[3]

The intersections of such powerful literary and political influences as well as experience of continental travel are vividly illustrated in what is possibly Lynch's first foray into print in 1881, 'La Puda de Monserrat', published in the same year she became London secretary for the Ladies' Land League.[4] In this debut piece, an autobiographical travelogue based on a sojourn in Spain, Lynch announced herself on the literary scene: 'My speciality lies in observing all things and persons', and 'I would prefer to write a book that would take a modest place in first-class literature than one which would stand first in a lower one' (26 November 1881, p. 139). Her rebel feminist position is revealed in a conversation about the French Revolution with a Marquis who, in response to her assertion that '[t]he Revolution would have been the noblest rebellion in the history of the world, had it been carried within the limits of humanity and justice' (3 December 1881, p. 149), accuses her of 'unwomanliness'. If this is Lynch's first publication, it is also the first in a pattern of provocations and indignation she stirred up during her short literary career, not least through her membership and active participation in the Ladies' Land League,

---

2. The Cantwells ran the Star and Garter hotel situated in D'Olier Street, Dublin.
3. It was a large family of sisters and step-sisters, Mary, Nannie, Virginia and Hannah Lynch followed by Teresa, Brigid, Patricia and Anna Josephine Cantwell.
4. 'La Puda de Montserrat', serialised in *The Shamrock*, 26 November, pp. 138–140; 3 December, pp. 148–150; 10 December, pp. 170–172, 1881. *The Shamrock Magazine: A National Weekly Journal of Irish History, Literature, Arts, etc* established by Richard Pigott, vol 1 no 1, 06 Oct 1866–11 Dec 1920. See North 1986.

which included a stint of editing and smuggling a proscribed newspaper.⁵ It is also striking that her literary and rebel feminist identity is asserted in a European setting, a feature of much of her fiction and non-fiction.

In fact, restlessness and continuous travel across Europe are defining features of Lynch's life and writing. Between her birth in Dublin in 1859 and her premature death in Paris in 1904, Lynch had traversed most of Europe. Starting early with convent school years in Paris and probably Coventry in England, governess posts in Ireland, journeys undertaken as a Ladies' Land Leaguer, her travels crossed multiple borders initiated through contacts and were often driven by financial necessity. Her sister Nannie held a governess post in Barcelona and it is clear that she was travelling to Spain prior to or even during her involvement with the Ladies' Land League. After a sojourn in London, breaking into the literary scene there, Hannah Lynch undertook an arduous sea voyage to Greece, residing on the Greek island of Tinos for several months in 1885 before moving to Athens and staying in Greece until 1887. Other places in Europe she visited and incorporated into her travel writing and fiction included various Italian cities (Venice, Verona, Lucerne), several cities and regions of Spain (Toledo, Tarragona, the Canaries, and 'Rebel Catalonia') and, in addition to Paris, a variety of regions and cities in France. London and Oxford in England feature in correspondence and travel pieces and of course Dublin and other areas of Ireland including County Mayo on the west coast and near Waterford where she held governess positions as a young woman.⁶ Her close friend, poet and essayist A. Mary F. Robinson took up residence in Paris in the 1880s and Lynch also

---

5. For example, she was accused of being unpatriotic for her critical portrayal of a west of Ireland community, her satirical portrait of W. B. Yeats and others who gathered at Katharine Tynan's literary salon in 1880s Dublin caused dismay as well as hilarity among these contemporaries, and her portrait of cruelties meted out to convent schoolgirls in her autobiographical novel, *Autobiography of a Child*, led to threats of libel by bishops.
6. See Binckes and Laing 2011.

made this city the closest thing to a permanent residence, dying there in 1904.

During this short life, the literary output of Hannah Lynch, travel writer, cultural commentator, novelist, reviewer, and translator was considerable, comprising

> ten novels, including her early, novel-length text 'Defeated', early short stories and novellas serialized in nationalist papers such as *The Shamrock* and the *Weekly Freeman,* one collection of short fiction, *Dr Vermont's Fantasy and Other Stories* (1896), and a series of uncollected shorter tales. Her final novel, *Autobiography of a Child* (1899), was first serialised in *Blackwood's Magazine,* and was later translated into French. Her diverse travel writings encompassed numerous articles and two full-length studies: *Toledo: The Story of An Old Spanish Capital* (1898) and *French Life in Town and Country* (1901). These were supplemented by a series of translations from French and Spanish. In addition to this Lynch was an active literary critic throughout her career. Her book-length *George Meredith: A Study* was published by Methuen in 1891, and she wrote extensively and comparatively on French literature while working as Paris Correspondent for the London literary review *The Academy* between 1896 and 1903. In between times, her witty and exacting critiques— as well as her passionate and generous endorsements—of figures in Irish, British and Continental literature appeared in periodicals and newspapers including the *The Freeman's Journal, The Fortnightly Review, The Contemporary Review* and *The Westminster Review.* (Binckes and Laing 2019, p. 7)

Her transnational fiction, novels and short stories, often feature an (Irish) New Woman character or characters and she also engaged with the diverse and often contradictory discourses surrounding this figure in the numerous cultural commentaries and reviews published across a range of periodicals, newspapers, and magazines.[7]

Ultimately, the figure that Lynch herself cuts is characteristic to some extent of the New Woman that so pervaded the press and popular fiction of the period, and the stories included in this volume are clearly autobiographical as well as tributes to Anna Parnell and her Ladies' Land League. These stories, 'Marjory Maurice' and 'A Girl Revolutionist', are also significant and valuable for the ways in which they reflect simultaneously a quest for Irish nationhood and new possibilities for young women at the turn of the twentieth century. Appearing in the nationalist story paper *The Shamrock* and a newly launched magazine, *Girl's Realm*, aimed specifically at a young female readership and offering alternative models of girlhood, the publications themselves reflect further these imbrications. Both stories offer insights into the contemporary press, its opportunities for women writers, but also limitations and constraints. Both stories might be described as examples of the female *Künstlerroman*, documenting Lynch's own apprenticeship as a feminist writer but, even more, a striking example of a late-nineteenth-century feminist activist and writer who is shaped by her experiences of journalism, editing, and newspaper publishing.

In short, these stories should be read in multiple contexts (land-war fiction, Ladies' Land League fiction, New Woman fiction) and intersecting fields of enquiry and scholarship, outlined below. Dana Hearne has highlighted how 'The Ladies' Land League led by Anna Parnell was extraordinary in many ways, not the least of which was the way in which it cut across divisions of social class, religion, and Irish nationalism' (2020, lvii). Offering rare fictionalised witness accounts of the activities of the Ladies' Land

---

7. Lynch's hitherto neglected life and writing has started to feature in numerous commentaries on late nineteenth-century Irish women's political activism and literary contributions. See Binckes and Laing, Ward, O'Toole, Foster, and Murphy, for example.

League, Lynch's stories illuminate further this intersectionality and should be read intertextually (see the Timeline above), especially as companion pieces alongside Anna Parnell's personal account of the history of the Ladies' Land League, *The Tale of the Great Sham*. Finally, as well as some of the earliest examples of Irish New Girl and New Woman fiction, the disappearance and recovery of these stories also highlights the riches of nationalist story papers and periodicals that await digitisation and further excavation.

The Ladies' Land League, Land-War Fiction and Popular Print Culture

Membership and participation in Ladies' Land League activities is a key co-ordinate on Lynch's timeline.[8] Elected as Honourable Secretary at the inaugural meeting of the London branch in February 1881, she, her sisters and half-sisters based in Dublin were all involved, featuring in newspaper reports on meetings and activities across both cities. As a movement that began in support of the imprisoned leaders of Land League in 1881, the Ladies' Land League became a powerful network of women from New York to Dublin, all over Ireland, to London and beyond to other cities where the Irish diaspora had gathered. They organised meetings and resistance to evictions, and sourced financial support for evicted tenants.[9] As Margaret Ward and other scholars who have revisited the fascinating short history of the Ladies' Land League have foregrounded, '[a]t its inception, the woman's organization was regarded by many as a significant marker in the campaign for gender equality' (Ward 2001, p. 75). Among those drawn to the nationalist cause and this particular crisis were a number

---

8. It is also key to the early writing and feminist activist lives of several women writers whose profiles have been raised across a range of studies on the Ladies' Land League. See Laird, O'Toole, McL. Côté, Urquhart, Ward, Hearne.
9. See Margaret Ward and numerous other discussions of the formation and practices of the Ladies' Land League.

of writers and aspiring writers. In fact Anna and Fanny Parnell, at the forefront of Ladies' Land League activities in Dublin and New York, respectively, were published writers and poets in their own right.[10] Based in Dublin, Katharine Tynan, another writer whose considerable oeuvre has received recent reappraisal, also participated in Ladies' Land League activities in a more limited way, while the poet Rose Kavanagh became involved once the Ladies' Land League took over running the proscribed *United Ireland*.[11] Hannah Lynch was also involved in editorial duties, ensuring the continued publication of this paper and enabling its distribution after it was proscribed. It is this aspect of her involvement that is so vividly portrayed in her short story, 'A Girl Revolutionist': 'The paper was all ready to appear next day, and the order had come from the Castle to seize it. The eight stereo plates were ready for print, and somebody cried, "Oh, if it could only be got to London, it could appear by Saturday"' (p. 194 in this volume). Anna Parnell's account of these events in her history of the Land League, *The Tale of a Great Sham*, offers a crucial context for Lynch's fictional account and parallel narrative:

> About this time the Land League newspaper, *United Ireland*, fell on our already well-laden shoulders. The government began a systematic oppression of this small weekly sheet. They seized the paper in the office and wherever else they could find it, and imprisoned the editorial staff. Notwithstanding these measures, the Ladies were able to get it circulated about the country very much the same as usual.

---

10. Anna Parnell's series of articles 'How they do in the House of Commons: Notes from the Ladies' Cage', was published in America in the *Celtic Monthly* (May–July 1880). A volume of her poetry was published in 1905 but her now iconic account of the activities of the Ladies' Land League in *The Tale of a Great Sham* remained unpublished until 1986. Fanny Parnell also wrote and published poetry and was the author of pamphlets on social and political conditions in Ireland. See the *Dictionary of Irish Biography* entries for both women.
11. For further details see Chapter One in Binckes and Laing, 2019.

> Then the printers were imprisoned also, and this put a stop to its being issued in Dublin, for printing was not amongst our accomplishments. … We not having acquired it, *United Ireland* had at last to be printed out of Ireland, in England and in France. It was sent over and circulated as before. (Parnell 2020, 122–3)

The 'unfeminine' and unconventional behaviour of the young revolutionary, Moya O'Connell, who sets off from Dublin to London on a 'midnight helter-skelter drive across the city', then a 'rush down to the boat' carrying the 'sacred plates of *Erin*' (p. 194 in this volume) in 'A Girl Revolutionist', and that of the Maurice sisters in Lynch's novella, who travel unchaperoned across and between cities, is indicative more generally of the metaphorical and literal boundary crossings of members of the Ladies' Land League.

It was a movement, as Tina O'Toole has noted, that marks a paradigm shift, when 'New' possibilities for Irish women began to emerge (2013, p. 69). A brief sample of some of these and other crossings foregrounds transnational literary and political networking and also gives a glimpse of other women writers whose prominence or visibility during this period has all but disappeared. London-based women writers, for example, became involved too, some with Irish roots and others who sympathised with and wished to give active support to the nationalist cause. These crossings facilitated some of the crucial feminist and literary networks for Lynch that began in Dublin and continued across to London and then Paris. Helen Taylor, step-daughter of John Stuart Mill, feminist and champion of Irish Home Rule and land reform, for example, supported the cause from London as president of the Ladies' Land League in London.[12] English novelist, essayist and artist F. Mabel Robinson, sister to Lynch's close friend A.

---

12. See the entry for Helen Taylor in the *Oxford Dictionary of Biography* online and O'Toole 2013, 84.

Mary F. Robinson, visited Ireland with Charlotte McCarthy and her father, the London-based Irish journalist, Justin McCarthy. According to some reports F. Mabel Robinson became actively involved in the Ladies' Land League and she turned some of these experiences into a novel, *The Plan of Campaign: A Story of the Fortune of War*, set after the period of land wars.

Literary representations of the Irish land war proliferated during the 1880s, and fiction written to address the crisis was 'produced very rapidly and with almost journalistic sense of immediacy' (Hansson and Murphy 2014, p. 7). As Hansson and Murphy go on to note:

> Despite their often semi-journalistic aspirations as early responses to current events, they are governed by the rules of fiction and cater for an audience that expects story, not primarily debate or social commentary. The fictional status of the works means that they cannot be understood as historical sources in any objective sense. Nevertheless, they provide information about attitudes, ideologies, responses and emotional reactions. They possess affective if not necessarily cognitive or ontological truth. (2014, p. 10)

While much of this writing, now identified as a distinctive subgenre, was penned by women, offering in many cases the opportunity to feature new possibilities for their unconventional female characters, few pay specific attention to the existence or activities of the Ladies' Land League.[13] Lynch's stories offer a rare and fascinating glimpse of these activities and practices. The longer and more detailed novella 'Marjory Maurice', for example, framed within the trappings of conventional romance and marriage plot fiction, offers a sketch of the busy Dublin Ladies' Land League office, presided over by Georgina Templeton, a fictionalised

---

13. See Hansson and Murphy, 2014.

version of Anna Parnell, and visits paid to the imprisoned Land Leaguers in Kilmainham prison.[14]

'A substantial body of land-war fiction appeared in periodicals and newspapers' (Hansson and Murphy 2014, p. 13), much of it never reprinted and subsequently forgotten. Digitisation has furthered the recovery of some of this material, although many publications still remain accessible only in library archives. *The Shamrock: a National Weekly Journal of Irish History, Literature, Arts* is one such publication and possibly the earliest of several nationalist papers Lynch contributed to during the 1880s. These include *The Freeman's Journal*, Boston-based *Donahoe's Magazine*, and William O'Brien's *United Ireland*.[15] *The Shamrock* was a weekly illustrated penny paper and, '[l]ike most story papers internationally', these penny weeklies were 'aimed primarily at a juvenile male readership, but also positioned themselves as family papers, and included fiction and regular columns intended for younger female readers as well' (Rains 2015, p. 265). The *Shamrock* was also, as Rains notes, 'an important vehicle for perhaps the single most important form of popular Irish publishing throughout the second half of the nineteenth century – historical fiction' (2020, p. 310). But in the 1880s, Lynch and a considerable number of other women writers contributing to this weekly were doing something different – mapping contemporary events and discourses – and their writing is distinctly feminist in tone and direction.[16] This is not surprising given that 'Lynch was not the only former Ladies' Land League member on board' (Binckes and Laing 2019, p. 30).

---

14. Lynch dedicates her novel, *Prince of the Glades* to Parnell. See Tina O'Toole's reading in *The Irish New Woman*.
15. The *Shamrock*, 'founded in 1866 by Richard Pigott, who also owned and edited the *Irishman*', consisted 'mainly of fiction and mildly educational articles' (Rains 2020, p. 309).
16. In 1881 the *Shamrock* was purchased by the Irish National and Newspaper Publishing Company, owned by the Land League (Benatti 2009 p. 569). Irish story papers were important and regular outlets for Irish women writers including Tynan and Mulholland (Rains 2015, p. 265).

Katharine Tynan and Rose Kavanagh along with Hannah Lynch contributed stories to a Christmas double number in December 1883/January 1884, 'Christmas on the Hills', for example, and most significantly, Rose Kavanagh, the poet and short story writer, was also the editor of the *Shamrock*.[17] As already noted, with this experience Kavanagh had joined the Ladies' Land League to help edit the proscribed *United Ireland* alongside Hannah Lynch: 'When the Ladies' Land League set about finding women substitutes for imprisoned journalists, [Kavanagh] offered her services, and Dublin Castle did her the honour of appointing a special detective to watch her'.[18] In such contexts the *Shamrock* would have been more than hospitable to Lynch's tale of feminist and nationalist endeavour as well as a defence of the Ladies' Land League.

The Irish New Woman and 'Marjory Maurice'

'Marjory Maurice' illuminates further Lynch's extraordinary literary, political, and highly cultured apprenticeship outlined by Katharine Tynan and glimpsed in 'La Puda de Monserrat', also offering a snapshot of the formation of the modern Irish New Girl/ New Woman in these contexts. The Maurice sisters, for example, are portrayed on the one hand as educated and accomplished young women in all the arts and conventions expected of their sex in the late nineteenth century. Literary quotation and allusions to classical and contemporary music as well as theatre are a feature of lively conversations between the sisters and their diverse friends,

---

17. Katharine Tynan recalled that 'I first met Rose in the days when Richard Pigott was editing the *Irishman* and Rose *The Shamrock*, a little weekly paper, in the same office in Middle Abbey Street', *Memories* (London: Everly Nash and Grayson, 1924, p. 163). There are several examples of Rose Kavanagh's contributions including a serialised novella, 'Clare Daly', that include attention to the land war, journalism, and publishing.
18. M. J. MacM., 'Rose Kavanagh', *Irish Press*, 23 June 1944, p. 2. For further details of this feminist, literary, and publishing nexus, see Binckes and Laing 2019, pp. 29–30.

and of the narrative more generally, demonstrating Lynch's own formative literary and musical education. But the sisters' talents are not confined to the private sphere, and their active involvement in politics through their membership and work with the Ladies' Land League challenges assumptions about gender roles, marking them out as distinctly modern and new. The negative stereotypes of New Women, often features of the contemporary popular press, are also foregrounded and questioned by channelling these perceptions through one of the most sympathetic male characters, the charming, accomplished, but initially prejudiced Cambridge-educated naval officer, Denzil Dalrymple: 'But bad as a meeting with a popular Land Leaguer would be, he remembered that there was something infinitely more objectionable to come in contact with in this eccentric island, and that assuredly was a lady Land Leaguer' (p. 38 in this volume). Expecting to find the Maurice sisters variations on the satirised figures of modern, political woman, a 'hybrid creation of agitation' (p. 38 in this volume), Dalrymple is forced to revise his opinions over the course of the narrative, undergoing a full conversion to the cause.

As well as offering positive images of modern young women, lady Land Leaguers in particular, in order to re-educate their male counterparts and the reader more generally, in 'Marjory Maurice', Lynch presents a 'slice of Dublin life', sketching out a social, geographical, political, and cultural map of 1880s Dublin and its environs. It is also a map that spatialises her own girlhood and young adult experiences and, more significantly, the intersections of the private and public lives of politically-engaged middle-class young women whose social interactions foreground surprising boundary crossings. Friendly with the superficial socialite Evelyn Handcock, whose family 'are noted for having all kinds at their house' (p. 38–9 in this volume) and whose circle includes lady Land Leaguers and British naval officers, the Maurice sisters traverse the city from fashionable 'Roiville' (Kingstown, now Dún Laoghaire) to the offices of the Ladies' Land League in Sackville Street, to their uncle's home in Leeson Street where they also live, to the church Morna Maurice frequents in Gardiner Street, and to Kilmainham prison. Scorned by Marjory's fickle fiancé and his associates for his roots in trade, the uncle's middle-class home is also a hospitable space for journalists, political activists, lady Land Leaguers and, in the end, admiring naval officers enchanted by the Maurice sisters. This 'social vortex' is indicative of the generic mix or 'vortex of genres' typical of fiction of this period.[19] *Roman-à-clef* romance, anti-romance and the marriage problem novel, satire, female *Bildungsroman*–often features of the New Woman fiction and land-war fiction–are some of the constituents of Lynch's serialised novella.

Through her portrait of the rebellious actions and characteristics of the Maurice sisters and their involvement in Ladies' Land League activities, and particularly her focus on Morna Maurice in the novella, Lynch offers a vivid and prescient vision of the New Woman and the New Woman fiction that became so popular and infamous at the *fin de siècle*. This figure, formally identified in contemporary discourses following the publication of Sarah Grand's iconic essay, 'The New Aspect of the Woman Question' in 1894, was already a feature of *fin-de-siècle* writing from the early 1880s. Olive Schreiner's 1883 *The Story of an African Farm* remains the prototype, establishing some of the central features of what became known as the New Woman fiction, and there are some striking parallels with 'Marjory Maurice', published a year later.

In contrast to the more conventional Marjory, Morna openly expresses her reservations about marriage: 'I have no disbelief in the beauty of perfect marriage. But when I look round I think it must be an ideal only, for I see nothing to justify our hope in it. … I don't think marriage broadens the sympathies; it restricts them to the home circle' (p. 77–8 in this volume). Such reservations are echoed by Georgina Templeton (modelled on Anna Parnell) who is equally sceptical about men and marriage: 'I never saw or read of any man

---

19. See Binckes and Laing 2019, pp. 42–66 and James H. Murphy 2011, p. 167.

worth falling in love with except perhaps Leonardo da Vinci' (p. 135 in this volume).[20] Morna's dedicated work for the Ladies' Land League means that not only does she work in the public sphere, in an office, but she also traverses Dublin, often unaccompanied, and, even more shockingly, late at night: 'She drives home every night at twelve o'clock from some kind of an office – often after that – on a fast car –' (p. 57 in this volume).[21] Equally outrageous, it is revealed that 'She let little Marjory go down to Cork on the night mail with another girl, of course somebody very disreputable. They travelled together and put up at a hotel like men, and drove round the country to prisons and evictions' (p. 58 in this volume).

The fate of both sisters, whose promise and vitality are thwarted in the end by failed romance and the subsequent death of Marjory, followed by Morna's retreat to the convent, can be read as a metaphor for the defeat and disillusion experienced by the members of the Ladies' Land League at their treatment by Parnell and the Land League more generally. The ending also anticipates the convention in many New Women fictions of closure in failure and often death. The most obvious predecessor to this narrative is Schreiner's *The Story of an African Farm* and it is possible that Lynch had read and was influenced by the novel before writing her own. Both writers frequented some of the same London coteries and literary salons, and they may have met

---

20. Georgina Templeton's reservations are voiced in a striking exchange with Marjory Maurice about marriage while they are busy with their work in the Ladies' Land League office: "I certainly cannot say I was ever particularly fascinated by any Irishman or Englishman I read of or saw. I find them a very ordinary and uninteresting collection of individuals. If you've written that letter I want you to direct the secretary of the Lodore Branch—post town, Cardoon, Galway—to send us all the particulars of the Murphy eviction case" (p. 137 in this volume). Lynch's narrative strategy (reminiscent of Flaubert's *Madame Bovary*) stages structurally the subversive intersections of the public and private spheres and challenges to the status quo that the Ladies' Land League movement represented.
21. There are echoes of Anna Parnell's unconventional behavior here. Katharine Tynan records her walking home alone from the Ladies' Land League office after midnight. See Hearne's introduction 2020, p. xxi and Tynan 1913, p. 80.

there.²² Certainly Marjory Maurice is as full of contradictions as Lyndall in Schreiner's novel. Marjory is at once an active member the Ladies' Land League contravening the rules of late Victorian feminine etiquette and at the same time ridiculously in love with a shameless cad (the novella's outspoken narrator laments this). Abandoned by said cad, Marjory literally wastes away and dies: 'She visited the Exhibition frequently, attended parties and concerts, laughed and chatted most brilliantly, and wished herself at rest in Glasnevin all the time. Of course it was noticed that she was a thought thinner, but only a thought, and who minds that in sensitive girlhood?' (p. 168 in this volume). The ending to Lynch's narrative is so abrupt, Marjory's decline is swift and not traced in detail, but clearly it is an act of self-destruction that intersects with and anticipates numerous examples of 'starving heroines' and self-harm in New Woman fiction of the period, including Schreiner's.²³ As Alexandra Gray highlights:

> Bodies which had been controlled, isolated and kept private, and which were now made sensationally public, came to symbolise damaged female subjectivity in the wound culture of *fin-de-siècle* fiction by women. These bodies are configured in New Woman writing through tropes such as self-starvation, excessive drinking and self-mutilation; they are figured both as inescapably subject to male oppression and, concurrently, as the authors of their own doom. (2017, p. 10)

---

22. That Lynch had encountered and admired Schreiner's novel at some stage is made evident in a letter to her friend Dimitrios Vikelas where she records giving a lecture on Olive Schreiner and Mrs Ward (April 1896, F.879 Vikelas Archive, Manuscripts, Archives and Special Collections Department, National Library of Greece).
23. 'Constituting the most spectacular case, in Victorian writing at least, of female teenage rebellion stifled by *anorexia nervosa*, its heroine Lyndall enabled Schreiner to introduce into narrative literature many of the feminist themes which, a decade later, would come to represent New Woman fiction generally' (Ann Heilmann ed., 1998, p. ix).

In addition to the patterns and tropes of self-harm identifiable in New Woman fiction, the specific historical and political contexts of Lynch's story, set during a period when 'the haunting spectre of the Great Famine still held a predominant position in the national consciousness' (Hearne 2020, p. lv), Marjory's anorexia can also be read as a 'Famine referent'.[24] In this way her death is doubly resonant, embodying disempowerment both in terms of nation and gender and, at the same time, registering Lynch's own feminist protest at these conditions.

Ultimately, for all her modernity and bold crossings of gender boundaries as a lady Land Leaguer, Marjory seems trapped by her own expectations of romance and equally, perhaps, the narrative conventions available to Lynch publishing her fiction in a popular 'story paper'. In fact, Lynch problematises at once the expectations of the romance genre she deploys by refusing happy endings or marriages for any of the central protagonists, and the aims of the *Shamrock* magazine, to provide 'fictional material of a stirring nationalist style'.[25] In this, one of her earliest published fictions, Lynch established a pattern of confounding narrative expectations that became a feature of several of her later works.[26]

Girl's Realm: Publishing Contexts, the New Girl Fiction and 'A Girl Revolutionist'

In her short story, 'A Girl Revolutionist', Lynch returned to her early and formative experiences of what can be described as feminist activism and disillusion with the male-dominated nationalist

---

24. Bonnie Roos's observations about Katharine Tynan's novel, *The Story of the Bawn,* and the use of anorexia as a Famine referent, and also a statement about 'an ambivalent and predominantly female symptom of both powerlessness and control', are particularly pertinent (2013, p. 342).
25. Rains 2020, p. 310.
26. *An Odd Experiment* or *Denys d'Auvrillac,* for example. Like her contemporaries, Lynch had to tread a fine line between marketability and establishing her own literary individuality.

project. Published in the magazine for girls, *Girl's Realm*, edited by the Irish writer and editor Alice Corkran, Lynch's tale offers a striking model of courage, adventure, and subversiveness. *Girl's Realm*, in contrast to *The Shamrock*, the older and more established nationalist story paper, was a London-based periodical, launched in 1898 targeting 'middle-class girls in its self-conscious modernity' and 'promot[ing] education, modern pastimes (such as photography) and physical activity for girls' (Rodgers 2016, p. 39).[27] Joining a flourishing market for periodicals and magazines aimed at adolescent girls cultivating notions of the New Girl and 'Girls' Culture', such as *Girl's Own Paper* and *Atalanta*, Corkran's editorial focus fostered a pursuit of heroic ideals and courageous action as models for the New Girl by publishing tales of adventure as well as articles on female role models and inspirational women.[28]

It is a story of heroic actions that include editing a proscribed paper and smuggling the stereo-plates out of Dublin – mapping Lynch's own experiences and anticipating the retelling of these actions in Anna Parnell's *The Tale of a Great Sham*. This tale offers for the girl readership not only a model for action and participation in public, even revolutionary events, but also the possibility of feminist activism through writing, editing, publishing, and distributing the banned paper:

> In revolutions there is no such thing as apprenticeship. There is something to be done, and the first person handy must do it, ill or well. A female editor of *Erin* was needed and Moya's apparent duty, though she had never written a line for print, was to seize this occasion. Undaunted, she sat herself in the

---

27. For more detailed discussion of Alice Corkran as editor and the aims and identity of this periodical, see Rodgers (2016, 2019) and Moruzi (2012).
28. See key studies by Rodgers, Mitchell, Moruzi and others listed in the bibliography in this volume for examples of the flourishing field of scholarship focused on nineteenth-century periodicals aimed at girls and young women and featuring the 'Girl of the Period' and the New Girl and the Irish New girl.

editor's chair, always forgetting to turn up that betraying blond pig-tail. Undeterred by the thought of prison or the gallows, she complacently killed off the Saxon in leaders, seemingly written in Saxon blood. Not capable of injuring a fly, she wrote with a pen fashioned of dynamite, and wiped out the British Institutions.

Never was *Erin* so virulent, so venomous, so spirited an organ. (p. 192–3 in this volume)

Lynch's tale illustrates for her girl readers one of the most positive experiences that the brief period of the Ladies' Land League offered to its members, as Anna Parnell noted herself in her *Tale of the Great Sham:* 'This running of *United Ireland* was the pleasantest part of all the work of the Ladies' Land League' (2020, pp. 122–3).

As a tale promoting revolutionary and rebellious roles for young women, 'A Girl Revolutionist' is also subversive on another level. The story of heroine Moya O'Connell, who dreams of freeing Ireland, is smuggled into a publication that promoted female courage, initiative, and even rebellion, but also tended to be supportive of the imperial project.[29] So, Lynch's story of revolution and literary endeavour was well suited to Corkran's aims on the one hand, but also strikingly at odds with the ways in which the colonial girl in particular was featured and positioned prominently in this and other magazines aimed at girl readers. Kristine Moruzi highlights the fact that in *Girl's Realm*, 'The colonial girl was seen as enjoying more provisional free space away from the constraints of British society while also offering the aspirational and imaginative possibility of colonial girlhood to British girls' (2019, p. 710). In contrast, 'A Girl Revolutionist' offers a short history and an explicit account of a rebellion precisely against colonial rule. The resignation expressed at the end of the story by Lord Fizelling, 'I dreamed of freeing Ireland. We all go through it and recover' (p. 196 in this volume), is ironically counterbalanced by the success

---

29. See Sunderland 2019.

of heroic Moya O'Connell in editing the outlawed paper *Erin* and smuggling out the stereo-plates in a trunk he has helped her, unwittingly, to transport.

Ambiguity and the absence of a definitive conclusion to this story, failed revolutionary dreams and an incomplete journey (which replicate to an extent the conclusion in failure of the 'Marjory Maurice' novella), was questioned in a letter to the editor by one of Lynch's admiring but puzzled girl readers. Alice Corkran included the ensuing correspondence in her editorial column, 'Chat with the Girl of the Period', and the question as to whether the story was finished or set to continue.[30] Hannah Lynch's wry response is worth quoting in full:

> The author of 'A Girl Revolutionist' is greatly flattered by N.D.V.'s desire for a more definite termination. But revolutions, like short stories, never have a proper ending. Their nature is episodic, and episodes and adventures rarely lead to anything. N.D.V. can end 'A Girl Revolutionist' to her own liking. There is a railway, a lord and London before the heroine. Would N.D.V. prefer a fatal accident, or marriage bells?

Corkran continues her column based on this correspondence, drawing attention to the features of the short story, noting that it is a 'fine art' and implying that Lynch, as one of its practitioners, is a model for her young readers and aspiring writers. Lynch was indeed an ideal model of literary and publishing achievement, having acquired, to some extent, 'a modest place in first-class literature' (p. 6 in this volume), the aspiration outlined in her very first publication. By 1899, the year her most successful work, *Autobiography of a Child*, was published, along with 'A Girl

---

30. The Editor, 'Chat with the Girl of the Period'. *Girl's Realm*, vol. 1, 1899, p. 648. My thanks to Beth Rodgers for alerting me to this correspondence in Corkran's column.

Revolutionist' and several travel and cultural commentary articles, she had extended her publishing profile significantly. Since her launch in the early 1880s in the more popular Irish nationalist story papers such as the *Shamrock Magazine,* Lynch had positioned herself across a range of markets, from Irish and American outlets with a focus on Ireland to a selection of prestigious British, French and American literary magazines and periodicals. Her novels and short stories were also published on either side of the Atlantic. Hannah Lynch's Irish girl rebel stories, 'Marjory Maurice' and 'A Girl Revolutionist' partially map this publishing history and trajectory from 1884–1899. Foregrounding feminist courage and endeavor, overshadowed by uncertainty, these stories capture in fiction a defining moment in the history of Irish feminism and glimpses of the membership of the Ladies' Land League, their actions and aspirations.

Note

The bibliographies that follow the two stories in this volume offer readers starting points for further exploration of Hannah Lynch's extraordinary life and writing as well as that of her literary contemporaries, (Irish) New Woman and New Girl fiction and publishing contexts, the Ladies' Land League and the political, social, cultural, and nationalist print contexts of late-nineteenth-century Ireland.

A Note on the Texts: 'Marjory Maurice: A tale of our times' and 'A Girl Revolutionist'

Both 'Marjory Maurice' and 'A Girl Revolutionist' have been transcribed from the *Shamrock Magazine* and *Girl's Realm* respectively with no revisions to the occasionally erratic and irregular punctuation and spellings (variations that might be printing errors have been indicated with [sic]). To retain the sense of reading 'Marjory Maurice' as a serialised story, volume numbers and dates have been included to reflect this. 'A Girl Revolutionist' was published with illustrations by M. Clarkson, which have not been included.

Marjory Maurice

BY HANNAH LYNCH

"Thou tiny pearl of demagogues,
Thou blue-eyed rebel, blushing traitor,
Thou sans-culotte with dimpled rose,
Thou trembling agitator."
Godiva: Brough.[1]

CHAPTER I

IN WHICH A DISTINGUISHED ACTOR IS INTRODUCED.

Towards the end of February, 1882, a young lieutenant in the navy was sent from Portsmouth to replace a brother officer in H.M.S. Adversary,[2] stationed then at Roiville, a very

---

1. Robert Barnabas Brough (1828–1860), playwright, journalist, and poet. 'Godiva' was first published in *Songs of the Governing Classes* (1855), a volume of poetry that launched 'an attack on the hypocrisy and inadequacy of the ruling class through satiric portraits of fictional aristocratic figures'. Cynthia Dereli, 'Brough, Robert Barnabas (1828–1860), playwright, journalist, and poet.' *Oxford Dictionary of National Biography.* https://www.oxforddnb.com/view/10.1093/ref:odnb/9780198614128.001.0001/odnb-9780198614128-e-3577.
2. H.M.S. Adversary: 'The Royal Navy always maintained some sort of presence in Kingstown, though the date of the establishment of a permanent guardship is unclear'. It was disbanded in 1904. (Pearson 1991, pp. 30; 152).

favourite port of navy men, and a well-known Dublin sea-side resort.³

The lieutenant was a young man of twenty-seven, of a decidedly prepossessing exterior, tall, fair, and slenderly but gracefully built, shyness in his manner that very nearly approached fascination. Candid, glad blue eyes, with a touch of childhood and sea-memories in their depths, and a bewitching softness in the long brown lashes, with their suggestive tendency to moistness, which was calculated to prove of brilliant effectiveness in love scenes of course; a great leonine crown of fair hair curling and waving thickly round his pale face, with a tinge of bronze in its fairness; full curved mouth, under a perhaps too delicate moustache, which feminine admirers had been known to describe as gold-tipped in thrills of delicious rapture; but it was just a little red and soft for masculine beauty. Then his nose was "quite too perfect"—hinting, as it did, at nervous susceptibility—in the ready dilation of its finished nostrils, and his forehead was something less bronzed from the rest of his face. His appearance, on the whole, was eminently distinguished, as should be the appearance of the scion of a good old Irish family, well-bred, as an equally natural consequence, with habits of the well preserved unoriginality of the habitual aristocratic lounger through life. Added to these striking points were a desirable amount of natural gaiety, an indestructible good-nature as an apology—ample, be it understood, considering the value of the article—for an unusual degree of intellectual force, and an individuality rather stronger than the neutral-toned intelligence of the average naval officer, who finds "girls" dooped bores, a morning champagne bath a rather good joke, and his own particular set the very finest produce in creation.

But Lieutenant Denzil Dalrymple was unconsciously a fellow of amazing parts. He was almost learned for a jolly tar, had actually

---

3. Roiville: thinly disguised reference to Kingstown, coastal town and harbour of Dunleary, renamed Kingstown in 1820 and returned to its original Irish name of Dún Laoghaire in 1924.

bought a copy of "John Inglesant," just published, and found it a little dull, but, by Jove, a wonderful book.[4] He read the quarterlies regularly, called himself an Agnostic, was proud of Cambridge, and was in the habit of asserting, gravely: "Come, now, you fellows really mustn't abuse Parnell. He and I were Cantabs, you know, and, fact is, I'm rather proud of Parnell, though he has broken with his order."[5]

He was also a violinist of exquisite proficiency, and cherished a profounder contempt for those unmusically inclined than even for those to whom literature and political debate were *terra incognita*. He knew enough of Latin to help him through an appropriate quotation, enough of French to draw him successfully through the mire of Zola, and the more graceful marches of Gautier without stumbling too inconveniently at the spicy or prurient bits which ought to satisfy the intellectual ambition of any healthy-constituted young man; found Ouida light and entertaining when not disposed for anything so massive as George Eliot, thought Scott and Dickens overrated but eminently preferred Thackeray.[6] He liked girls when they were "nice" and not gushing; under such favourable circumstances he could be induced to play his violin with touching and subtle charm, he could look into a pair of eyes, irrespective of shape and colour, as ardently as any unmatrimonially-disposed Irishman, hint unutterable emotions with a look, a sigh, a half-sentence, or a bar of music, and carry on the interesting game of flirtation as dangerously and as successfully as any other handsome young man. This, we know, is a delightful and admirable propensity,

---

4. *John Inglesant* by Joseph Henry Shorthouse, published in 1881. It has been described as a 'philosophical romance'.
5. Cantabs: members of the University of Cambridge. Charles Stuart Parnell attended Cambridge from 1865–9 but did not finish his degree. See the *Dictionary of Irish Biography* for further biographical details.
6. Dalrymple's literary tastes and opinions echo Lynch's own, articulated in later fiction and reviews. Émile Zola (1840–1902), Théophile Gautier (1811–1872), and Ouida, pseudonym of Marie Louise Ramé (1839–1908), constitute the more modern and controversial writers on this reading list.

and it would be clearly absurd to be too critical in the case of a charming and good-natured fellow like Denzil Dalrymple. His very name lends distinction and claims that easy and graceful latitude I am sure none of my readers are disposed to deny him, especially when we take into consideration the fact that he is returning to his native land after an absence of seven years.

One word more, and my reader will know more about this young gentleman than he probably should himself, as he stood watching a couple of sailors lift his luggage into the pinnace which was waiting for him at the jetty in the light of a chill February morning, when a faint grey mist lay over the sea, hiding the western coast from view, and the sky was weighted with low-hanging rainclouds.

He possessed no relatives but a married brother, with whose wife he was not on exceptionally good terms, and a mythical grandfather, whose fate was still an unsolved problem, since he had mysteriously disappeared from the north coast of Ireland, leaving behind him a large collection of Irish crystals, supposed to be of inconceivable antiquity, and a still more learned collection of beetles, which Denzil suggested should have been presented to some public institution. Besides his pay he inherited a property that brought him three hundred a year, which income tided him pretty safely, but not extravagantly, over the shoals and quicksands of early manhood, enabling him to indulge, not so moderately as might perhaps be imagined, in the usual amount of vices, considered to be necessary to the perfecting of virility. He always smoked the best cigars, cultivated an amicable weakness for good champagne, and—but why expose the delightful vagaries of such a brilliant adornment of H.M.S. Adversary?[7] He was no worse

---

7. Names of naval ships serving as guardships in Kingstown during the late nineteenth century included HMS Audacious, Invincible, Iron Duke, and Vanguard (Lowth, Cormac F. 'Guardships at Kingstown', *Journal of Research on Irish Maritime History,* http://lugnad.ie/guardships/). Dalrymple's post on the HMS Adversary has both comic and political overtones, highlighting a

than the best young men we meet every day, and a great deal better than a good many. If he could be as grave as a senator, as audacious as a roué, as careless as a boy, as changeable as a girl, as cold and sad mannered as a philosopher without pedantry or learning, as emotional as a woman, passionate or gentle as a child, I do not believe his moods ever seriously injured anyone. Given with his surprising facility for adopting the humours and ways of others, the versatility of his attraction and talents, his personal grace and beauty which had in it something of distinction, a little more genius of a higher order than that which brings more popularity, the same means of exercising his power and influence, the same taste for conquest, there was no reason why he should not achieve a fate fashioned on that of Alcibiades.[8]

"I'm just in nice time for a wash before breakfast," he cried, jumping in and remembering his gloves in order to help himself to a little brandy. "By George, I don't know when I felt colder," he muttered, tilting back his head as the flask reached his lips, and then critically surveying the cold, grey outline of buildings edging the harbour, "Have you Lieutenant Brecknock here now?"

"Yes, sir, I'm thinking you'll find him a little seedy this morning," answered a sailor, with a sense of humour respectfully restrained, "Me an' me mate had the lifting of him over to the 'Adversary' last night, an' mighty sprung he was, too."

"I'm not surprised at that, and it didn't much matter, I suppose, if you hid his razors. I believe Roiville is a very jolly station. It looks cold enough now," said Dalrymple, ruefully.

"I don't know one as wouldn't be very sorry to have to leave it, sir," was the cheerful rejoinder.

---

tongue-in-cheek awareness of naval names and an ironic foreshadowing of both his initial reservations about Lady Land Leaguers and indeed the ideals of Irish nationalists.

8. Alcibiades: a reference to the brilliant, successful fifth-century Athenian general who also makes an appearance as a character in Shakespeare's *Timon of Athens*.

CHAPTER II

DALRYMPLE MAKES A CHARMING ACQUAINTANCE.

A few days later Lieutenant Dalrymple had made arrangements to occupy rooms in the house, where his former friend, Arthur Brecknock, lodged, in Marino-terrace.[9] The rooms were not elaborate for a fellow of his pretensions, but they were at least expensive enough to justify his exulting in the notion of exclusiveness; and then there was a magnificent view of the sea and a distant hill, on which all the tones and semi-tones of the seasons lingered in varying expression. But I will do Lieutenant Dalrymple the justice to say that he cared nothing at all for these things. The sea, from the sight-seeing point of view, was naturally an exhausted subject with him, and a charming young man really cannot be expected to take an interest in landscape.

One morning the friends were sitting smoking at the open window. It had been raining heavily earlier, but as the rain cleared off and the sun gleamed delicately over sea and land, the colours of young spring shone out in vivid clearness. Just the sort of morning to attract lazy young men to an open window, sheltered, of course, behind by the warm firelight, and to bring active maidens from their homes.

"Look, Dal, there's a tremendous flame of mine," cried Brecknock, with that short, contemptuous laugh masculine intelligence thinks proper to adopt on such occasions, pointing with his cigar, as he laughed, to two young ladies who were walking on the narrow pathway leading to the pier.

The pathway lay exactly opposite the window, at which the officers were seated, and Brecknock took their appearance as a bit of worn-out homage to his own attractions.

---

9. Marine Terrace: a fashionable address in Victorian Kingstown (Tom Conlon, *Victorian Dún Laoghaire: A Town Divided*. UK: The History Press, 2016, p. 81).

"What an infernal lot of trouble those girls do give themselves in running after us. Dooced little fools, too. By Jove, I wish they wouldn't bore a fellow so. The tall one walks well, doesn't she? That's some girl she's picked up with, to keep her in countenance."

"Who is she?" asked Dalrymple, carelessly, as he bent slightly forward to look at them.

"Evelyn Handcock—a damned fine girl, with as handsome a pair of eyes as you'd wish to see, and a pot of money, if any fellow were inclined to settle down. 'Pon my word, I think I ought to go down after her. That's what's she's expecting. Do you see her looking up at me now? Watch now and you'll see her slacken her pace, and then she'll stop altogether to examine a sea-gull or see if the Adversary hasn't changed its position. Fine fun it is, watching all their little dodges; but, by Jove, I think I ought to go down to her. You've no idea how good-natured she is; quite the jolliest girl out."

"Then take me down, too, and introduce me," cried Dalrymple. "I'm game if you're not."

"I've overtaken you, Miss Handcock," was Brecknock's somewhat obvious statement, as he lifted his hat and looked sideways into the pleased and smiling face of the lady.

"Oh dear me! How you surprise and startle me," cried Miss Handcock, with a too palpable assumption of innocent amazement. "We didn't think you saw us; did we, Charlie?" she asked of her companion.

"How do you do, Miss Mason," said Brecknock to the girl appealed to, "Let me have the pleasure of introducing you to my friend, Lieutenant Dalrymple."

"So pleased to meet any of Lieutenant Brecknock's friends," simpered Miss Handcock, in the usual way. "I do so hope you will like Roiville, Lieutenant Dalrymple. It's very pleasant when you get to know a lot of friends, isn't it, Mr Brecknock?"

"Quite the jolliest place in the world. Shall we walk towards the Pier?"

"Yes, but I do wish you would take us out for a row, Mr Brecknock. There's nothing so pleasant as rowing on a rough sea, don't you think so, Mr Dalrymple?" said Miss Handcock, with her affectation of divine appeal.

Dalrymple thought her certainly one of the handsomest girls he had ever seen, but not his style. She played with her eyes too much and smiled more than was necessary, besides her method of flirting was coarsely shallow and unladylike. His intellect was sufficiently refined to make him wish for a little of it in the woman he meant to amuse himself with, and beyond her mere physical beauty, which was striking, he found nothing else of interest about his friend's friend.

"It is a good idea, I think," he replied, cavalierly, looking as he spoke across the sea.

Evelyn perceived the absence of cordiality in his manner, but was not abashed by it. Dalrymple was singularly handsome, while her admirer was a little old, redder in the face, and stouter than was exactly elegant. On the whole, he looked too homely beside his companion for further notice, and with the ready decision of young ladies devoted to an object than which none, perhaps, requires a greater amount of promptitude in judgment and decision, she resolved at once to transfer her maiden affections to the more fitting object, and to spend her maiden exertions in urging him to a similar decision as regarded herself.

Evelyn Handcock was very nearly beautiful. She was of medium height, with a voluptuously perfect figure, which would probably become too massive in middle age; her face was full like a child's—fat her enemies might describe it—and tinted with nature's finest delicacy; full, red lips, very suggestive to the male mind of kisses; large, prominent, blue eyes, sparkling and attractive, without much expression, and thick, dark-brown hair, which made her neck and face the fairer, curling richly round her forehead in provoking grace. A lover would have found the contrast of the little dark rings above her brilliantly white neck adorable.

With a slight manoeuvre she managed to secure Dalrymple for herself as they turned towards the pier, leaving Miss Mason and Brecknock to what consolation they might draw from each other.

"I do so love the Adversary that everyone connected with it seems quite too perfect in my eyes. I was at one of the balls last month; it was so madly jolly. You can't think, Mr. Dalrymple," she smilingly observed.

"Indeed I can think, Miss Handcock. A ball is pleasant enough for the first hour, but after that I am generally bored to death."

"Only think! How droll! My papa and my brother are no different. They find balls awfully jolly. Don't you like dancing?"

"I enjoy a waltz with a good partner occasionally. Would that entitle me to say I liked dancing?" he asked, with his inattentive look.

"Oh, there's nothing worth living for if it isn't waltzing. I adore it, especially with one of you fellows of the Adversary in uniform."

Dalrymple smiled grimly, and thought he could find something more heavenly than dancing with her in or out of uniform.

"You're a rum sort of girl, you are," drawled Brecknock, who had overheard her remark, and turned, with his peculiar sideway-look. "You're quite fetching, you are, I know, but you mustn't go it too hard with Dal. He's the best fellow in the world, but that won't prevent my getting jealous."

"Oh, now, Lieutenant Brecknock, it's quite too absurd, really, to hear you talking like that. I'm sure Mr Dalrymple is disgusted at such silly nonsense," cried Evelyn, in affected protestation.

"I think you ought to be flattered, Brecknock. Miss Handcock meant to convey that she took an interest in the Adversary fellows for your sake; at least I am forced reluctantly to presume so, since the interest existed before our introduction, and the contemplation of that fact must for ever [sic] shatter my peace of mind. I wonder did I leave any girl in Portsmouth in love with the whole Invincible for my sake. I wish I did."

"Nonsense. I'm not in love with the Adversary for Mr. Brecknock's sake," pouted Evelyn. "In any case, I'm sure I could never be in love with Captain Leighton. He's quite shocking and ugly."

"Poor Leighton. He is a kind of brute, I admit; but, then, so many fellows are brutes that one gets accustomed to it in no time," said Dalrymple, gravely.

"I know one navy man who is more of an angel than a brute," murmured Miss Handcock, audaciously.

"Meaning Brecknock, of course," added Dalrymple, by no means blind to her meaning.

"Oh, Mr. Brecknock, indeed! He is very nice, but he is too red and stout to be an angel. He's not at all my ideal of an officer. He should be tall and fair; fair men are so madly charming and aristocratic looking. No one can tell what colour his eyes are, and I do so like eyes of decided colour—like blue, for instance. I perfectly rave about blue eyes in a man."

"This sort of thing some fellows find delightful," Dalrymple thought, "but to me it is simply disgusting. The girl is an abominable flirt, only tolerable on account of her beauty."

Aloud he said:

"And I adore blue eyes in a girl. My ideal woman has lovely dark brown hair with the faintest bit of pink in a brilliantly fair face and a pair of lips enough to set a fellow mad. Do you like her?"

"How droll—how charming—how awfully jolly! We both admire each other's style," said Evelyn, blushing becomingly.

Their conversation, though less exclusive, was no less enlightened and cultivated during the row, when Evelyn insisted on relieving Dalrymple with happy little screams and laughter and all the rest of nonsense which usually accompanies such elegant efforts.

At parting, she invited both men to five o'clock tea at Eden Park on the following evening, announcing for the occasion the greatest novelty of the times—two lady Land Leaguers, who had promised to come, old schoolfellows, she explained, and rather nice girls.[10] The invitation was accepted.

(To be Continued.)

Vol. XXII – No. 951
Saturday, January 3, 1885: 213–215.

CHAPTER III

A TEA FIGHT.

Not without much surprise at the seemingly questionable society into which his friend was introducing him, Denzil Dalrymple, having completed his toilette, sat smoking before the fire while awaiting Brecknock's appearance from his room.

He admired Parnell as he admired Lord Randolph Churchill, as something in politics original and distinct.[11] He regarded the leader of the Irish cause as fully entitled to the respect and admiration of any Englishman or West Briton,[12] because, however objectionable or erratic his theories might be, he was certainly a statesman and a gentleman, but Mr. Parnell's followers were quite another thing. If called upon to meet any of them he would unhesitatingly decline to do so. He had some vague notion that those men usually entered society in their native land heralded by brass bands, banners, and rowdy orations; he probably even

---

10. Eden Park: near to where the Lynch/Cantwell family lived in Newtownsmith, Glasthule, https://localwiki.org/dl/Cantwell_Lane
11. Lord Randolph Churchill (1849–1895): Influential and divisive figure in the Conservative Party, particularly interested in Irish politics and father of Winston Churchill.
12. West Briton: a disparaging or derogatory term used to describe an Irish person who shows particular admiration for or affiliation with England or Britain.

pictured them as adorned with green sashes and rosettes, perhaps even in knee-breeches and corduroys, by way of patriotism in costume. But bad as a meeting with a popular Land Leaguer would be, he remembered that there was something infinitely more objectionable to come in contact with in this eccentric island, and that assuredly was a lady Land Leaguer. If it were not for the spirit of adventure, which inspires a stranger in Ireland to find an inexhaustible excitement in getting drunk on Irish whisky, he would certainly have refused. After all there might be some fun in it. If the girls were not vulgar or aggressively political, there was really no reason to assume that they would turn out much worse than the ordinary English woman's-righter, except that there would be a stronger amount of excitement in watching how this hybrid creation of agitation would conduct herself in society.

But his philosophic conclusion did not lessen in his eyes the strangeness of the class of people with which Brecknock had got himself mixed up with.

"How the devil did you manage to pick up with this set, Brecknock?" he asked, as his friend appeared, drawing on his gloves.

"With Evy Handcock, you mean? Oh, why, I say now, she's right good value," drawled Brecknock.

"There might be a second opinion on that subject too. But don't you see they must be mixed up with deucedly objectionable people when they have Land Leaguers at their house."

"I don't know, Denny. I met Evy in Grafton street one day with one of these Maurice girls, and, by jove, she was very fetching I can tell you. I shan't object to meet her," said Brecknock, helping himself to some whisky and water.

"Probably," returned Dalrymple rising. "But you must admit they are queer acquaintances for Miss Handcock, if, as you say, she's of good family."

"Oh! the Handcocks are noted for having all kinds at their

house.[13] They go in for that sort of thing, and I suppose it amuses them. I fancy, though, that Evy is a little bit soft on a fellow mixed up with the Land League. She likes to keep him on hands in case she can't get one of us fellows."

"She does us too much honour, indeed, to put us in competition with some rowdy Irish politician," sneered Dalrymple.

"Oh, he's not rowdy. Leighton met him at Handcock's, and he says you'd mistake him for a gentleman if you didn't know. He dresses remarkably well and shows uncommon good taste in the selection of his cravat. I wish that fellow of mine could induce me to say the same of him. Just look at this hideous object, Denny."

"Oh, come, it's just five. It'll do splendidly," cried his friend, impatiently.

It was after five when Brecknock and Dalrymple were ushered into Mrs. Handcock's drawingroom. Tea was going on, and the lieutenants were eagerly welcomed.

"How very charming that you have been able to bring your friend," said Mrs. Handcock, approaching with extended hand and a smile announcing all the amiable ease of stout matronhood.

Evelyn saw them enter, and nodded familiarly from the end of the room, where she was sitting with an evident admirer.

"He is a journalist or something in the newspaper line, I don't exactly know what," whispered Brecknock. "You'd be surprised, but he's a rather good sort of fellow, and is quite the thing in a smoking-room, I can tell you."

Dalrymple stared at the journalist, a tall, thin man, slightly stooped, with thin, dark hair worn away at the temples; a thin face, adorned with a dark beard, finely-cut features and eyes of uncertain blue, whose lustre had probably exhausted itself in something other than hard study. In repose, he looked grave and

---

13. The striking social mix hinted at here is a feature of a later, Dublin-set novel, *The Plan of Campaign* (1888) by English writer Mabel F. Robinson, Lynch's contemporary, Ladies' Land League associate, and friend.

interesting, but when he spoke his face lit up beyond recognition with humour.

Dalrymple wondered what would be the next kind of article pointed out to him. He shook hands with Miss Handcock, and seated himself beside her. After the necessary preliminaries, he gazed round the room, as he leisurely stirred his tea. He did not see anything like his ideal of a lady Land Leaguer there; he was, consequently, a little disappointed. He saw Brecknock being introduced by Mrs. Handcock to a striking-looking girl, with light-brown hair and large pearl grey eyes. The eyes, fringed thickly with lashes of a darker shade than her hair were the most strangely spiritual eyes he ever saw, the effect of which was deepened by the firm, pale face, with its expression of restrained sadness and endurance.

He was conscious of looking a little longer at the girl than was exactly permissible by social law when his neighbour addressed him gaily.

"What do you think of my friend, Marjory Maurice? She's awfully good value," said Miss Handcock, pointing to a slim, golden-haired, blue-eyed girl. "I wouldn't advise you to fall in love with her because she is a furious red-cap,[14] and happens to be engaged as well to a charming boy."

"She certainly has a witching little face. But what do you mean by calling her a red-cap, Miss Handcock? Surely she is not the lady Land Leaguer you spoke of?"

"Her politics only lend piquancy to her beauty," observed the journalist, speaking in a low, slightly-hesitating utterance, and drawing his hand slowly through his beard. "In her heart of hearts she admits that she is enamoured of Lord Randolph Churchill. I entertain hazy views of cutting him out some day, and would undoubtedly do so tomorrow if I could make up my mind to go in for Parliament instead of adventures."

---

14. A revolutionary or republican, associated with the French Revolution, an allusion in this case to activism with the Ladies' Land League.

"I should introduce you, Lieutenant Dalrymple, to Mr. Power," Evelyn laughed.[15]

The gentleman bowed somewhat coldly. Neither seemed impressed by the introduction.

"It's rather difficult to meet with adventures nowadays," was Dalrymple's original remark.

"Ah, yes. I would suggest the impossibility in this part of the globe. I refer to the East. I've met with some very tough adventures there, I can tell you."

Evelyn stooped forward and called to the golden-haired young lady, who at once approached.

"You've had enough of mamma, Marjory. Come and join us now," Miss Handcock said.

When Dalrymple applied the word "witching" to Marjory Maurice, he best described her. She was as slender and as supple as a reed, with a figure whose movements were almost as expressive as her face. Everything about her was unrestrained, and wild, and bright, from her little arched feet to the gold-crested head where the curls waved and rippled round the palest and tiniest face in the world, a pair of eyes like wide-cupped pale forget-me-nots, whose long lashes seemed to have caught the lingering sunlight, and under a delicious little *nez retroussé* smiled a childish mouth of vivid scarlet: Truly "a tiny pearl of demagogues."[16]

Dalrymple stared at her in blank astonishment. He had been building hopes on a woman of the Louise Michel type, with

---

15. Mr Power: one of many journalists to feature in Lynch's and other Land War fiction. He is most likely modelled on Edmund O'Donovan (1844–83), who was a family friend of the Lynch/Cantwell family (Binckes and Laing 2019, p.139) and who is alluded to in Lynch's *Autobiography of a Child*. Frank le Poer Power (1858–84), another journalist and war correspondent, accompanied O'Donovan on assignment in 1883. Lynch appears to merge both adventurers by anecdotes of exploits and name; both were deceased by the time she wrote the novella.
16. 'Tiny pearl of demagogues': from Brough's *Godiva* included in the epigraph to the novella (p. 27 in this volume).

vibrating voice and full assertive gaze; a woman merged into a kind of hybrid hysterical manhood, whose chief accomplishment would lie in her power of talking people down.[17] And here sat before him a delightful bit of petulant girlhood, one could fancy a forest-bird and bringing the sunshine right into the heart of the woodiest depth; a mere negation of sorrow or care much less political aggressiveness; toned in nature's vividest colour: blue and white, and gold and scarlet.

Her dress was simple and picturesque: black, with something fluffy and shining about it, a deep lace collar, and neck cut low like an old-fashioned miniature, lace ruffles to match the collar, and silver bracelets; not much to describe but infinitely effective to look at.

Somebody had moved towards the piano. There was a brilliant cascade of variations, during which time Dalrymple scarcely removed his eyes from the little face where expressions chased each other in bewildering rapidity, till at last the features grew into a brief, merry, sad quiescence.

The young lady moved from the piano, and Brecknock crossed the room to where his friend sat beside Miss Handcock.

"Oh, do play, Mr Dalrymple," cried Evelyn. "You've no idea how I adore to hear a man play. It's so different from women, and so perfectly charming."

"I'm sorry I can't oblige you, Miss Handcock," said Denzel, curtly. "I can't play."

"Then I must have been remembering some other fellow, but I really thought it was you. I'm very glad you don't play, Den," said his friend, tranquilly.

---

17. Louise Mitchel type: 'The mention of 'Louise Michel' and the 'redcap' drew upon various mocking or threatening images of revolutionary women in circulation'. These images were a feature of political cartoons in publications including *Punch* and *Funny Folks*. Lynch is invoking a particular cartoon in this description, 'In Bad Company', where Anna Parnell is depicted as a Louise Mitchel type (Binckes and Laing 2019, p. 50).

"Why?" asked Evelyn, with a look of surprise.

"Oh, well—ah—you know it's such a bore having to listen to a fellow playing tunes," returned Brecknock, tranquilly.

"Then I'm very glad I haven't been playing for you, Mr. Brecknock, if that's the way you feel," observed Marjory, in mock gravity.

"Oh, come now, Miss Maurice, you mustn't be too sharp with us poor devils of fellows. I didn't mean that at all, you know. A fellow looks so stoopid at the piano, but you girls—'pon my soul, it's awfully nice, it is. I'm sure I could listen to you playing tunes forever."

"You'd be asleep in half an hour, and ready for murder in two. My playing, as Evelyn could tell you, is more remarkable for brilliancy and crash than for accuracy. I really doubt if your sanity would stand the test of Schulhoff's 'Carnival de Venise'. Would it, Evy?" asked Marjory.[18]

"You really mustn't say such things of yourself," murmured Brecknock, languidly. "Do try me with the 'Carnival de Venise'."

"However desirous you may of being tried, I must have some consideration for the rest of the company," laughed Marjory.

"As for me I'm always ready to listen to any kind of music, provided I am not asked my opinion on it afterwards," said Power, quietly, "I only know three airs: 'Patrick's Day', 'The Wearing of the Green', and 'God Save the Queen'.[19] Beyond that I can't tell one from another."

"Then you're not as bad as my cousin," said Marjory. "Of course, we don't acknowledge him because he's a low-class Conservative, but I sometimes have a dash with him on the sly. Some months ago

---

18. Julius Schulhoff (1825–1898), 'Carnaval de Venise', Op. 22: Bohemian pianist and composer. The conversation probably draws on Lynch's own knowledge of the composer and piece as an accomplished pianist herself.

19. A provocative mix of nationalist airs, the British national anthem, 'God Save the Queen' and Irish nationalist songs, 'Patrick's Day' and 'Wearing of the Green'. See note 118.

there was a Land League oration near Tuam, and he was passing by with two friends of his who played a delightful trick on him. You can fancy what his ears is [sic] when they could persuade him into believing that the band was playing "God Save the Queen," when it dashed frantically into "Patrick's Day." Of course they told him that a loyal county inspector couldn't pass by without lifting his hat, and he did so and was loudly cheered."

"I remember when I was in Persia, there were two tribes encamped close to one another, but still the deadliest enemies. I fraternised with one and as a natural consequence was bound to hate the other. But the difficulty was to distinguish between them," said Power, stroking his beard in great gravity. "Their costume was precisely similar except for the turban, and the only difference was that one turned out the yellow side of the scarf and the other the red. How is a man without an eye for colour morally capable of taking in such a nice detail as that?"

"I could imagine the difficulty," said Denzil. Brecknock felt the fellow was a bore, and moved away, but then, remembering a good story of his own, turned back.

"You're political, Miss Maurice," he drawled, slowly, looking perfectly grave. "You must remember when Trelawney was Chief Secretary, don't you?"[20]

"Oh, we all remember Trelawney's time," rejoined Evelyn, with her effective smile.

"Quite so. Well, the Adversary was then at Roiville, and just after his appointment Prince Antonio died, and when Trelawney was coming, and as the Government he represented was the means of stopping the men's allowance of rum, the sailors were pretty glad to see him, I can tell you. What do you think was his first remark? 'What,' he asked, as if he were in the House, 'are your masts broken? Oughtn't you to have them mended?" When they brought him to the armoury chamber, he looked around as if he

---

20. The anecdote is unclear; the Chief Secretary alluded to as Trelawney could be based on William Edward Foster who held the position in 1880.

had never seen such a thing before, and asked, 'Does one man sit in this place all by himself, and keep all that armour cleaned?' If you ever come down to the Adversary, Miss Maurice, I'll show you the kind of work Trelawney, a Cabinet minister, wanted to know if one man had to get through. When he was going to luncheon he only found some porter and ham. That's all we gave him, and an ironical cheer, when we saw him go away with a hungry and miserable face."

"Confess now, Mr. Brecknock, have you not stretched your imagination a little in the story of the broken masts?" laughed Marjory.

"Perfectly sure I haven't. I appeal to Denny. He'll tell you he's heard it before."

"Oh, anything Brecknock says that is not about himself is sure to be Gospel truth, Miss Maurice," said Denzil, thinking he could remember afternoon parties at which he had felt more bored.

"Why didn't you bring Frank Harston, Marjory?" asked Evelyn.

"His friend Reville asked him down to Meath for a couple of days' coursing," said Marjory, with a vivid flash in her eyes, which momentarily deepened their colour, and the faintest suggestion of a blush, which was a mere wave of shell-coloured pink, from throat to brow, subsiding in happy light.

"That's some fellow she is in love with," thought Denzil, watching her in keen admiration.

"I must drag Morna away from papa. I am sure he is boring her to death," cried Evelyn, jumping up.

Denzil followed her movements and saw her stop beside the pale girl with thick, light brown hair and eyes of pearl-gray, passionless, sad, and tender like a soul's. He at once hoped she was going to introduce him to her. The little one had just made some outrageously witty remark to a reply from the journalist, at which he laughed heartily, but was busy all the time wondering how it would be to find eyes full of such unconscious and spiritual appeal in their clear depths looking at him. For a moment he even forgot Marjory's fun and laughter, and rose, moving towards Mrs. Handcock, simply because she was near Evelyn's companion, whose tones he thought he would like to catch.

Evelyn saw his manoeuvre and called him. Her friend, she knew, was perfectly safe from a flirtation, and she attributed Denzil's apparent curiosity to a natural desire to inspect more closely anything so peculiar as a lady Land Leaguer.

"This is Miss Maurice, a politician, weighed with care and gravity, who has only deigned for a moment to bend to the lower frivolities of life. She's quite an imposing personage, so you must be careful how you address her, Mr. Dalrymple," she laughed.

"I've just approached her with a bated breath and downcast eye, I assure you, Mr. Dalrymple," put in Mr. Handcock, rubbing his hands, as he always did at his own jokes. "You must swear your belief in the uncrowned King of Kilmainham if you don't want to be shot."[21]

Miss Maurice returned Dalrymple's bow with a grave smile, and a full look of her large, grey eyes. They were even more beautiful than he had thought, and their impressiveness was increased by the slightly massive structure of her head and features. She was certainly the most tranquil-breathing and distinguished-looking girl he had ever met. Everything about her suggested stateliness and perfect goodness. She was not a girl, but a woman and a lady, made for all the resources of woman's deepest tenderness and highest purpose.

He felt at once he would have been proud to say such a woman was his sister or his mother, but in the name of all that was wonderful how did she come to be a lady Land Leaguer. It only remained now to hear her voice. Was it sweet?

"Mr. Brecknock tells me you have only lately come to Roiville," she said simply.

---

21. A reference to Charles Stewart Parnell, often referred to as the 'uncrowned king of Ireland'.

There was nothing in the remark, but the sweet graciousness of the tone and look thrilled him. No mere society acquaintance amongst women had ever before addressed in such simple gravity. They usually simpered and blushed, and used their eyes in deference to his profession no doubt, but he did not like it, because he had learnt to cherish a hope of purer womanhood than the fast officer-hunter. Not that I do not believe that the girl who degrades herself by running after military and navy men, as we must admit too many of them do in that class, is not, with all her unwomanly subterfuges and manoeuvres, infinitely too good for the men themselves as a very general rule; but for the girl's own sake it is nevertheless a saddening fact to contemplate that women are educated into believing that any fool or scoundrel, adorned with a uniform of some sort, is a being set apart for the distinction, the emulative efforts and worship of the whole sex.

He took the vacant seat beside her and asked her if she were really a lady Land Leaguer. She answered in the affirmative, with the same grave, earnest look.

"But surely, you don't—excuse me, Miss Maurice, but am I to understand that you go about the country making speeches in the open air, or anywhere else, accompanied by bands and banners and wretched mobs, unwashed and smelling of tobacco and worse?"

"I don't do that, because it is not necessary; or rather because I would not be able to do it," she answered, simply. "I should not care to make speeches; but, if it were necessary that I should do so, and I felt confident I had sufficient ability to say anything worth listening to, I would not hesitate."

"Good gracious! And you wouldn't feel degraded within sound of those atrocious bands?"

"Not in the least. Why should I? If the people take delight in the bands, how could their pleasure possibly degrade me?"

"Why you might as well say that, because the people take

delight in whisky and porter, you would not be degraded to find yourself in the midst of a *drunken mob*."

"The one is sin of a loathsome nature, the other the best form of national pleasure and expression," she said, a little sternly.

"And your pretty sister?" he asked, looking over at Marjory.

"Oh! she is simply light and sunshine. Work has nothing in common with her."

"And what kind of work can you do?" he asked eagerly, not meaning to be impertinent.

"That would be a difficult question to answer, Mr. Dalrymple." Denzil was silenced, and soon left Eden Park.

(To be Continued. – Commenced in No. 949.)

Vol XXII. – No. 952.
Saturday, January 10, 1885: 229–231.

CHAPTER IV

FIRST IMPRESSIONS ON ONE SIDE.

Out in the shivering February evening Denzil Dalrymple drew the deep collar of his outer coat round the silk scarf which sheltered his neck, and then proceeded to light a cigar which was a pretty good one, though not the orthodox perfumed Manilla usually allotted to fashionable heroes. His friend followed his example, and they walked in silence down the short, dark path with its many skeleton trees, touched to misty purple in the evening light, leading to the main road between Roiville and Duntley.[22] Crossing the road they followed the railway line down to the sea. Here Dalrymple paused, apparently

---

22. Duntley: Dalkey, a suburb of Dublin.

with the object of lighting another cigar, looked across the sea vaguely, and said:

"By Jove! It's wonderfully curious, after all."

"What? Not the sea, surely?" suggested his friend, in amiable surprise.

"Well, no, not the sea, exactly. I was thinking of those girls."

There was a pause, after which Brecknock answered:

"Well, there were a lot of them, certainly. Are you referring to the bright-faced one with all the golden hair?"

"I am speaking of the Maurices. I remember somebody telling me over the other side that these Land League women dressed nearly like men or the Nihilists, in double-breasted coats and holsters and jerry hats, some of them carrying pistols in their pockets, and meeting in a place they called an office, where they smoked cigars and cigarettes and drank brandy and water.[23] Then, again, I was fully persuaded that they were not ladies, or even women of average intelligence or education, certainly neither womanly nor pleasant. By Jove! what remarkable mistakes we do make."

"'Pon my soul, Denny, I rather like them. I think them very nice sort of girls, the little one especially; the tall one is—well, just a little too heavy and serious, don't you know. A fellow doesn't always know what to say to that sort of woman. But the blue-eyed one, by George! but she's a stunning fetcher, she is."

There was another pause, during which Denzil was wondering why the eldest Miss Maurice looked so sad and grave. He thought he would assuredly like to know something more about her.

---

23. The description invokes another cartoon. 'Published on 12 February 1881, the cartoon is simply titled, 'The Ladies' Land League' but carries a much longer subtitle: 'Alarm has been created by the formation of a Ladies' Branch of the Land League. Thus far, however, nothing more serious has resulted than in the adoption of a charming land league costume for the members, the effect of which was tried at an 'At Home' given by Mrs Rory of 'The Hills', Tipperary', *Funny Folks*, p. 44. (See Binckes and Laing 2019, p. 190, fn 39).

"I wonder are they often at Handcock's," he said, aloud.

"Never met them there before. They used to be long ago, very much; but that was before the Land League commenced. I daresay our fair Evy would have dropped them there if it weren't for that political fellow she's hankering after. I wonder he wasn't there this evening."

"What kind of fellow is he? The one with the well-chosen cravat, I suppose you're alluding to?"

"Oh, he's well enough, gentlemanly and all that, if he weren't such a damned, infernal prig. He's one of your leading-article talkers, and, of course, a nuisance."

"Where do these girls live? In Roiville?" asked Denzil, with unconscious eagerness.

"No, somewhere in Dublin, I believe. Faith, I know as little about them as you do yourself. By Jove, that's a fetching little one! Marjory! What a dooced queer name, too. You missed the best of her when she walked right into that fool of a newspaper man. The fellow is well enough, but he sometimes overdoes the lies. According to his own account, you know, he might have married one of the Infantas when he was in Spain, and Don Carlos borrowed a few pounds from him which he never paid back."[24]

"If Don Carlos did condescend to borrow a few pounds from an Irish journalist, I certainly credit the fact that he did not repay them," laughed Dalrymple. "I was rather interested in the fellow, and shouldn't object to meet him again."

"Oh, so do I like him; but a fellow can't be expected to stand everything. For instance, how can he swallow in one night a

---

24. Additional details about the journalist Mr Power that flesh out further his likeness to the exploits and adventures of Irish journalist and war correspondent Edmund O'Donovan, whose diverse and often exotic and sometimes dangerous, travels included Spain at the time of the outbreak of the Carlist uprising in 1873. For more information see the *Dictionary of Irish Biography*.

proposed elopement with an Infanta—Power on a mule riding frantically down one of those infernal Spanish mountains with the colours of Spain in his hand?—that's one of the feats we are asked to believe he performed—actually saved the colours of Spain! Then the Arabian princesses; his five Eastern wives, his camels, and that extraordinary candlestick with which he wrote his letters and stabbed any unfortunate devil that disturbed him in the vein of composition. I went to see him sometimes. I'll bring you some day to see him and get him to tell you the story of his attempted marriage with an Eastern mountaineer's daughter. It's rather good, you know."[25]

"Is he a friend of the Maurice's?"

"Well, yes. He swears by them in some of his moods; but that goes for nothing. He offered to introduce me once, but I didn't care about it, even had I believed he knew them as well as he pretended."

"He struck me as being a little soft on your friend, Miss Handcock."

"Oh, that's his way; he's soft on every woman he sees for the first time, till he meets another."

"You might guess that of him from his face."

They let themselves in and went to their separate rooms. Denzil sat down before the fire and fell to musing. He began to wish he had met more women with the grave gracious manner of Miss Maurice. He was not in what is precisely termed a sentimental mood. He was really not given to sentiment, but he had what is rarer than is admitted in men, a reverence for womanhood in its best and purest sense. I have said he was a good hand at flirting, but he did not really enjoy the pastime, for he never remembered having respected any of the women with whom he

---

25. Some of the tales of O'Donovan's adventurous and romantic life, doubted by Brecknock in conversation with Dalrymple in Lynch's story, are alluded to in an obituary published in *United Ireland* and reproduced in the *The Pilot*, December 22 1883, p. 2.

flirted. With any experiences that had gone further than mere surface-depth, he did not at any time care to dwell on. Even now his impressions were vague enough. It only occurred to him that if men were more thrown in contact with women who did not give rise to ideas of love, or badinage or marriage, it might be better for them by creating within them a capacity for more generous judgment and finer aspiration than the general run of men are capable of.

There was certainly something grand about that girl with the strange eyes, perhaps even severe. Her way of life and manners proved at least that they were all wrong about the organisation when they represented the women as unsexed, and vulgar, and aggressive. Again he dwelt lingeringly on the memory of her look and eyes, and resolved to call soon on the Handcocks.

CHAPTER V

ON THE OTHER.

Having entertained no previous misconception of officers with whom contact was calculated to alter, Miss Maurice and her sister had no communications of a particularly exciting nature to make during the short train journey to town.

Marjory lay back in the carriage shivering pleasantly beneath her muffling, and occasionally taking a bird's-eye view of the dark landscape they were hurrying past, at which her sister sat gazing in placid contemplation, then falling back among her wraps with another of her childish little shudders.

"I wish Frank could have been with us," she said at last. "I wonder how he and Neville are getting on down in Meath. My own old Frank, I hope he is lonely for me. I can see him going up to his room to-night and shaking his head into the looking-glass talking to himself: 'Come, now, Frank, it's an infernal shame the way you've behaved to that poor little girl since you came down here. It is, 'pon my word, you've only sent her a paper and a few lines. Come, now old boy, you really must write her a decent letter to-night to cheer her up.' That's the way he talks to himself I know."

Morna smiled on her caressingly.

"What did you think of the new lieutenant, Morna? I found him – *parfait*," she cried, with a slightly foreign gesture.

"He is quite a boy," said Morna, casually.

"How so? You'd be capable of thinking an aged, toothless old man a boy if he hadn't a beard. I've no doubt if you were asked abroad what you thought of the chief you'd say he was a mere boy."

"Oh, no. I've no doubt Mr. Dalrymple looks younger than he really is. I was referring more to himself than to his appearance. He is very boyish."

"Dear me! you astonish me," said Marjory, in mimicking gravity. "And in the name of goodness, Morna, how can you tell that he is boyish? I hope he didn't propose to turn a somersault in the drawingroom for your edification, or perhaps he invited you out to watch him play leap-frog with his sylph-like friend."

Morna laughed and shook her head.

"No, but he attacked me at once about the Ladies' Land League, and, considering we are utter strangers, that was a slightly boyish proceeding, you'll admit."

"I hope he didn't express, like Lieutenant Brecknock, a burning desire to shoot us out into the sea in a torpedo," and [sic] laughed Marjory.

"Not exactly, but he cherished a particular horror for the bands and banners. He spoke very pathetically of their degrading influence. I was sorry you were not there to give me a histrionic description of your visit to Cork, and the one brilliant effort at oratory you made."

"He is very handsome, isn't he? Quite like what you read of," observed Marjory.

"Quite. And what is more to the purpose, he seems to have some brains, unlike his friend, who is hopelessly foolish."

"Nonsense, Morna. Arthur Brecknock is real value. He told me a splendid story about Trelawney, and I'm going down to the office this evening to tell it to the girls. I prefer him to Mr. Dalrymple, because he is more in keeping with the exquisitely absurd type of the officer—like the fellow in *Play*.[26] You remember: 'So-and-so of ours is quite literary, you know; he reads books and that does for us all. When one fellow in the regiment reads we say we all read; you know it comes to the same thing.' I could fancy Arthur Brecknock saying the Adversary was quite literary, because his friend, Dalrymple, happened to read a book."

They were at the station by this. The girls walked hurriedly from the platform, Morna a little in advance to call a cab. Arrived at Leeson-street, Marjory jumped out and ran inside.

"Is dinner ready, Kate?" she asked in her clear gay voice.

"Yes, miss. Your uncle is home."

She rushed into the dining-room where her uncle was sitting, and threw her hat on a chair with a petulant little sigh.

"Did you enjoy yourself, Marge?" asked her uncle, looking up from his paper.

"Very much, Morna looked pale and grave, a little worried. I fancy. Power was there; he is coming to see us tomorrow."

Morna, standing before her glass, thought too she looked pale and grave, and smiled and shook her head in vague negation.

Vol. XXII. – No. 952.
Saturday, January 10, 1885: 230–231.

---

26. *Play:* possibly an allusion to Gilbert and Sullivan's operetta *Patience*. Reginald Bunthorne, the principal male character is named in conversation later in Lynch's narrative.

CHAPTER VI

EVELYN HANDCOCK GIVES LIEUTENANT DALRYMPLE SOMETHING TO THINK OF.

Two days later Denzil left the United Service Club earlier than his friend, whom he left half dozing over a cigar and his afternoon allowance of brandy.[27]

He sauntered a little aimlessly towards the station with a half-formed notion of calling on the Handcocks, and before he had quite made up his mind to do so found himself in the train and on his way to Roiville. This is the kind of impulse to which many of our actions are due, and if the sequent occurrences happen to prove momentous we call it Fate.

"After all she is not a bad sort of girl, had she stuck bravely to those Land League friends of hers," reflected Denzil, as he walked from Roiville Station to Handcock's house in Eden Park, fully persuaded that it would be extremely discourteous and improper on his part if he did not call soon on Evelyn, and equally convinced that his present determination was only the result of the friendly feeling and interest he felt towards that dashing young lady.

Evelyn was, of course, delighted to see him, and welcomed him with a smile of evident satisfaction.

"It's really too bad mamma and papa are both out, but they are sure to be back soon if you wait," she said.

Somehow Dalrymple was not sorry for the prospect of a *tête-à-tête*. Why should he differ from other fellows? He sat down with evident alacrity, and flashed a look which might mean a great deal on his companion.

"It's all the pleasanter, isn't it?" he asked.

Of course, Evelyn blushed and turned aside her head, leaving

---

27. United Service Club: The Hibernian United Service Club was founded in 1832 at the Royal Barracks as a private club exclusively for officers in the British Navy and Army stationed in Ireland.

his eyes to rove in mild discretion over the little dark rings staining the brilliant fairness of her neck. Then she fixed on him a look of captivating appeal and simplicity.

"Is it really pleasant for you?" she urged.

"Can you doubt it?" he rejoined.

"It is so nice to feel pleasant?" she suggested.

"Awfully nice, especially when one is pleasant," he smiled.

But this was becoming altogether too abstruse, and already Dalrymple was feeling fatally bored.

"I don't know when I enjoyed myself more than the other evening," he said.

There was nothing in this remark calculated to lower Evelyn's spirits, and her rosy lips parted in one of her usual waves of silvery laughter.

"Wasn't it awfully jolly?"

This was her form of sentimentality.

"Quite so. I was very much interested in your friends, the Miss Maurices. They are really very nice girls, all things considered."

This was not quite so pleasant, and Evelyn's face changed. It is true the praise was expressed with much implied patronage, and if repeated to the girls themselves they would have found no reason to feel flattered by it, nevertheless the tranquil blue of Evelyn's eyes darkened angrily and her lips tightened over her white teeth.

"Yes, indeed, considering their low tastes and questionable surroundings," she said, bitterly.

"You think the Land League very low, then?"

"Oh, the men are all low-bred *sans culottes,* and the women— oh!" she cried, with an effective shudder, "if you knew, Mr. Dalrymple, what class they are—uneducated, unwomanly, unsexed, and vicious; a lot of brutal and vinegar-faced old maids, who go about the country doing most disreputable things."

"For instance," suggested Denzil, coldly.

"If I know! Making low open-air speeches, I suppose; running away from Constabulary men, carrying banners, and jumping over ditches to witness evictions, travelling about the country and staying in hotels—lots of things."

"But Miss Maurice told me she did nothing like that," he said, quietly.

This fairly exasperated Evelyn. She turned on him, pale with anger.

"Then, I'll tell you what she does do. She drives home every night at twelve o'clock from some kind of an office—often after that—on a fast car"—[28]

"Good gracious!" cried Denzil, with a visible start, "I thought ladies did not drive on cars even with an escort."

"Oh, the ladies of the Land League do," sneered Evelyn.

"But are there no gentlemen to see them home?" he asked, shocked.

"Apparently there are no men, or, at least, the men shirk the duty. It is absurd to connect the idea of a gentleman with anything so low."

"Come now, the head of the whole thing is a gentleman, and a very fine fellow, too," interrupted Denzil shortly.

"Oh, he," pouted Evelyn.

There was a pause, during which Denzil was thinking angrily of the fast cars at midnight, and he asked:

"And do you mean to tell me that that pretty and attractive little girl is allowed to drive about on outside cars? Have they no male relatives?"

"Yes; they've an uncle, but much can't be expected from him, you know; he's only a Dublin trader—a rich merchant. But that is nothing."[29]

The reference to Marjory's beauty infuriated her, and she directed a blow which she knew would tell on his aristocratic feelings.

---

28. Travelling unchaperoned on 'outside cars' and working outside the home became clear indicators of New Womanhood in fiction of this period.
29. The sharpness of Evelyn Handcock's snobbery was endured by Lynch whose own family wealth was acquired through trade (See Binckes and Laing 2019, p. 8).

"Ah! How was I to know they were in business!" he said, frigidly.

Yet, notwithstanding the extreme unpleasantness of associating anyone in whom he was interested with anything so gross and unpardonable as trade, he could not help himself from remembering with admiring regret the sweet and gracious presence of Morna Maurice. He thought it hard to connect the owners of such lovely eyes with midnight drives on fast cars, and again the thought of the uncle in trade thrust itself upon him.

"I used to think Irishmen at least knew how to take care of their women folk," he said, unconcernedly, as he shook off the remembrance of Morna's eyes. "He must be a very coarse-grained fellow."

"No, I rather like him. He's awfully good value. He'd take care of the girls if they'd let him. He used to see them home at first, but Morna would not let him after a bit. It's Morna that's to blame for it all. She let little Marjory go down to Cork on the night mail with another girl, of course somebody very disreputable. They travelled together and put up at a hotel like men, and drove round the country to prisons and evictions."[30]

The picture thrilled Denzil with a shock of disgust throughout his whole aristocratic being. He sat looking silently at his carefully trimmed nails and decided the girls could not be worth the trouble he had intended to take to know more of them. That little golden-haired, blue-eyed Marjory, with all the distinctive marks of aristocratic breeding about her, her charming appearance and witching ways, to think of her with no chaperone or escort travelling in a night train and engaging a room in a hotel! There could clearly exist no genuine refinement where such things were possible.

He shrugged his shoulders as if in self-rebuke, and, looking up, met Evelyn's half angry, half scrutinising gaze.

"'Pon my word, Miss Handcock, it is a very advanced and curious state of affairs. The young ladies appeared so unlike all

---

30. Anna Parnell's *The Tale of a Great Sham* details these activities briefly mentioned in Lynch's story.

you tell me of them. There is no danger of your following their example, I hope."

"I! I don't think there is anything about me, Mr. Dalrymple, that could lead you to imagine me incapable of unsexing myself," she returned haughtily.

For a moment Miss Maurice's grave quietude and unconscious grace of bearing and expression rose before him in striking contrast with the ways and manners of her friend, and his intellect and individuality were strong enough to enable him to ask himself in irony if a girl might not sin against all the proprieties by driving at midnight unescorted and on outside cars, and yet preserve a sweeter womanliness and dignity than the maiden carefully veiled and guarded in the protecting shadows of home. Whether was it fairer, nobler, more womanly to be following a misguided sense of duty, he reflected, than like the fast and silly flirt beside him, set herself to flatter an eligible young man in her mother's house with disgusting frankness and parade up and down outside his window? The women of his order, he knew, thought nothing degraded in flirtation which was likely to conduce towards a good match.

When he contrasted such theories with Miss Maurice's assertion that she was prepared to do what she personally disliked if it would lead to good, he began to think it quite possible to find something more objectionable in the aristocratic paths of life than the peculiar ways of patriotism-infatuated women—if one could only get over the prejudices of the thing.

He looked into Evelyn's candidly-simpering and eager face, and smiled vaguely.

"You are quite right, Miss Handcock. I didn't, of course, mean to infer that it would be possible you could ever adopt the eccentric habits of your interesting friends you have just described."

Evelyn was again restored to radiance and satisfaction. After that she believed he would not be likely to inquire again for Morna Maurice.

"But Morna is a very nice girl, all the same," she said, patronisingly.

"Oh, undoubtedly," he answered, carelessly, thinking of the wonderful pearl-gray [sic] eyes, full of sad and mysterious dreams under their thick, shadowy fringe of dark-brown. Of course, he was not going to bother himself any more about the girl for all her sad eyes and pale, firm face; but then he thought he would just like to look into the eyes once more, only to assure himself that he had caught their expression quite accurately. But the pictures of those car-drives filled him again with angry disgust. And the meetings reported in papers—common, vile newspapers—and the office, and the degrading, mannish life and some horrible trader of an uncle, all standing blots on his memory. Would he trouble himself any more about her?

(To be Continued – Commenced in No. 949)

Vol. XXII. – No. 953.
Saturday, January 17, 1885: 244–246.

CHAPTER VII

MORNA AND MARJORY AT HOME.

Marjory Maurice sat reading one of her lover's letters before the fire while waiting for her uncle and Morna. It was just dinner-hour, and Marjory was lying back indolently in an arm-chair, where her golden curls rested, like a tangled cluster of floss silk, shining with all their shades of baby-flaxen and yellow and silvery gleams. If there were one thing about Marjory more lovely than all else, it was surely her hair, which shone like a wonder. Her hands held her letter, but her eyes—like dreamy forget-me-nots—were fixed on the blazing firelight. How fair and sweet and radiant she looked, musing on her lover, and sometimes glancing at a written word of his.

Suddenly she heard a knock, and hastily thrust her letter into the little silk pocket of her embroidered apron. She looked up brightly as Morna entered.

"How white and tired you look!" she cried, leaning forward and resting her chin on her hand. "Uncle is not in yet, but dinner is ready. Of course, he'll be back when everything is spoiled, and make himself black with passion. You ought to lie down till he comes. Shall I draw over the sofa, or would you prefer an arm-chair?"

"I'll lie down, thanks. I am tired, Marge. I feel as if I'd like to go to sleep for a month," said Morna, drawing her hand across her forehead wearily, and standing with one foot on the fender and her head resting against the mantelpiece.

"Do you know that you are getting delicate? I never saw you looking so bad," said Marjory, with a look of concern.

"Well, I don't look brilliant to be sure. I don't feel quite strong lately. I must get a tonic, and next Sunday I mean to spend the whole day sleeping."

"And in the name of goodness what do you want staying so late in the office?[31] Must you go back after dinner?"

"Yes, I haven't got through half my work. By the way, if you go to the pocket of my ulster you'll find a few autographs for your album," said Morna, moving towards the sofa, on which she stretched herself with a long, deep sigh.

"You heard from Harston to-day," she said, when Marjory returned with the envelope of autographs. "I saw a letter from him on the hall-table when I was going out this morning. Is he coming up soon?"

Marjory performed a dance of her own composition before answering, and then cried:

---

31. 'The Ladies' Land League was formally established on the 31st January 1881 at a meeting held at 39 Upper Sackville Street, Dublin, the headquarters of the Irish National Land League. During the first ten months of its existence the Ladies' Land League co-existed with the Land League and its office in an upper room of the same building' (O'Neill 1982, pp. 123–124).

"He'll be up to-morrow by the mid-day train. His nose was nearly bitten off by the frost. Fancy poor Frank with the end off his distinguished nose! By the way, you seem to forget that Power is coming this evening."

Morna opened her wide eyes indolently on the small face made half light and shadow in the uneven firelight.

"I had forgotten all about it. It is too bad; I wanted you to do some work for me."

"Directing No-Rent Manifestoes and licking on stamps, I suppose. Well, perhaps, Power will help me. By way of inducement I'll invent something more about my Lord Silchester."

"What is all this nonsense about, Marjory?" cried Mr. Maurice, entering the room unperceived, and laying his hand on her slim shoulder in a heavy caressing gesture. "Dinner is coming up now."

"I'm trying to show Morna that she is morally bound to stay away from the office this evening—in the first place, because she looks fagged, and in the second, because Mr. Power is coming to tea," returned Marjory.

"You do look done up, Morna," said Mr. Maurice, looking casually toward the elder girl, as he unfolded his napkin, when they were at table.

"If Mr. Power comes soon after dinner I can promise to devote two hours to his entertainment," said Morna, laughingly, as she rose and took her seat.

"Is all chance of arresting the woman at an end now?" asked Mr. Maurice in mock-gravity.

Marjory nodded her head.

"Quite," she answered in the same tone.

"I met Hamilton in Sackville-street at luncheon hour. He mentioned he would call this evening at seven, as he knew that would be the best hour to catch you both at home," observed Mr. Maurice, complacently.

"What! My adored Herbert Mercer," cried Marjory, with an

assumed look of ecstasy. "I think, uncle, you'll have soon to tell him that I am languishing in a secret and hopeless passion for him, and I regard him as an admirable specimen of the first gentleman in Europe."

"He wouldn't believe you. He says you are satirical, and he believes you mimic him."

"But couldn't you persuade him that that is only a mask of love!"

"Faith I couldn't, Marge. Love, masked or unmasked, lies lightly on your soul, as I've a mind to tell that youngster on the warpath down in Meath."

Mr. Maurice was really fond of Marjory while he contented himself with the fixed belief that her sister was the very best girl in the world. But she was merely grave and good and saintly to asceticism—a fine and beautiful influence in a household assuredly; a soothing presence, kindly and sweet, especially in hours of trouble, and only severe towards herself. But Marjory, with her shining eyes and golden head, was sunshine, a flower, a very fairy arrested in mortality, and giving stability to the memories of fairyland. She was all that is bright and lovely in nature—like a swift-winged hum of her brightness and loveliness. No one dreamt of asking if she were good or wise; no more could be asked of such mortal radiance but mere existence, the sight of which gushed all around into laughter, and sunshine, and irresponsibleness. Three years before the girls, left orphans, had come to live with him as their natural surviving guardian. He was a lonely bachelor, whose devotion had hitherto been exclusively divided between his business and politics. Marjory's presence in his dull and gloomy house had a marvellous effect on him. She never entered the room when he was there that he did not look up in a kind of vague and wondering pleasure, puzzled how such a slim creature of merriment could perpetually feed on her own inward joyousness; perplexed with the doubt that the sunshine could remain with no touch of genuine responsiveness near it. He never looked on her face or listened to her fun without laughing, and sometimes, under its influence—which he described as acting on a lonely life like his as a bottle of champagne on a care-worn mind—he was painfully apt to forget the exigencies of age.

"There is a ring; I suppose it is Mr. Hamilton," said Morna. "Lizzie, you had better light the gas in the drawing-room at once. Bring up tea there as soon as Mr. Power comes. Marge, you go up with uncle first, and I'll come up afterwards. I really am too tired for talk just yet."

"You know how physically unable I am to entertain anyone till I've had my after-dinner glass of punch," said Mr. Maurice. "So run on up, little one, and you'll have a delicate opportunity of explaining your tender condition towards him. If he refuses you, you may mention, of course, that pistols and coffee for two will be ready down here whenever he likes."

"Heavens! Picture the redoubtable Herbert Mercer Hamilton a gory corpse, and I, tragically unconscious, with dishevelled hair, flung beside him," said Marjory, with her hand on the door-handle, as she turned on them a grave, wide-eyed look.

"I'll damp your prospects there—see if I don't—when I tell Herbert Mercer the brutal alacrity with which you pictured him dead," shouted her uncle after her.

"She gets wilder and wilder every day," said he to Morna, shaking his head with an approving smile, "What will settle her? Will marriage, do you think? For, faith, her engagement has not lent her an iota of womanly dignity. If you heard the mad pictures she gave me of her married life in the future last night, 'pon my word, you wouldn't wonder at my despair at seeing an ounce of sense knocked into her little head."

He sighed, and looked into his glass as though he entertained some hazy notion that the vexed problem might somehow be found solved in the depths of warm whisky and water.

"Isn't she happier as she is?" said Morna, lying back wearily in the arm-chair before the fire and closing her eyes. "You and I can do all the thinking and sense for her till she is married, and then the care of keeping her life bright and unclouded will devolve, not quite exclusively, on Frank Harston's shoulders.

"But if she becomes a mother, Morna. Won't she want sense then?"

"Oh, you know, I never intend to marry; so I can very well devote myself to their children. Somebody would want to do so, because the children would surely come to grief if left in Marjory's or Frank's hands," said Morna with a warm smile. "I hope he'll be good to her," she murmured, opening her eyes dreamily.

"Good to her! Damn it! I'd like to know why he shouldn't," cried Mr. Maurice, rising and finishing his punch. Placing his empty glass carefully on the table, he added: "He'd find me a tough customer to deal with if he brought a cloud into her bright life."

Left alone, Morna lay looking at the firelight, thinking chiefly of Marjory's engagement. She liked Frank Harston well enough. He was cheerful, good-humoured, young fellow, of average good looks, a gentlemanly appearance, and tolerable means. But was he the husband for Marjory? She could not help remembering certain little traits about him which she distinctly disliked. Although he was as brainless as the usual run of tennis-party young men, horribly dandified, she knew he had a good deal of worldly wisdom. For all his openness there was something in him which did not suggest candour, and throughout his frivolity she once or twice caught a hint of the falsity of his moods. Marjory was a summer bird, and she could not help feeling worried about her future. If Frank Harston devoted more time to his profession—which remained, so far, a standing matter of study—and less to lawn-tennis and parties, and the perusal of light literature, there would be a brighter promise ahead, she thought.

CHAPTER VIII

IN WHICH THE READER IS INTRODUCED TO HERBERT MERCER HAMILTON.[32]

When Mr. Maurice entered the drawingroom he found Marjory kneeling on an arm-chair of dull amber plush, which showed out the outline of her slender waist encircled in a black silk jersey, while her head rested over the back of the chair under her fair clasped hands. It was not an orthodox attitude for a young maiden discoursing discreetly with a member of the opposite sex, but it suited Marjory admirably, and who could afford to be critical when the girl has "eager eyes and yellow hair,"[33] and wit enough to disarm the subtlest criticism? Certainly, Herbert Mercer Hamilton was not the man to be critical under such extremely soothing circumstances.

He was sitting exactly under the ray of her bright, blue glance, and though he was not in love with her, he certainly thought her the most charming little witch in the world, and regarded her engagement to that young popinjay without brains or sense as sweetness wasted on the desert air. He rose when Mr. Maurice entered the room with a listening look towards Marjory which meant to convey to her that this was only to be regarded as the

---

32. Herbert Mercer Hamilton, already introduced, appears to be loosely based on an amalgam of figures, possibly the editor of *United Ireland*, William O'Brien, or William O'Donovan, the younger brother of Edmund O'Donovan whose alias, 'Dr Hamilton', hints at affinities. 'William O›Donovan (1846–86), journalist and Fenian, was born 28 July 1846 in Dublin. […]. Like Edmund, he was a highly proficient linguist, and before he was 20 was sent to Paris by James Stephens to help John Mitchel (qv), who had become financial agent of the American Fenians in Paris (1865). Under the name 'Dr Hamilton', William acted as interpreter for the messengers sent with money for Ireland'. Bridget Hourican, 'Edmund O'Donovan', *DIB*. https://www.dib.ie/biography/odonovan-edmund-a6712#co-subject-A
33. '[E]ager eyes and yellow hair': a quotation from Robert Browning's 'Love among the Ruins' (1855).

briefest of pauses in their delightful conversation.

"I am hearing an amazing story about an ex-Chief Secretary, Mr. Maurice," he said.

"Ah! yes, but you know I don't believe a word of it," nodded Mr. Maurice.

"What! Doubt the word of an officer of her most gracious Majesty's Royal Navy!" cried Marjory. "Uncle, I'll have to send private intimation to the Castle that you should be reasonably suspected."

"Oh! if you were going to hold out such a frightful threat as that I suppose I had better retract and swear that your friend, Lieutenant Brecknock, is immaculate as far as his word is concerned. Am I interrupting an interesting confession, Hamilton. I know this niece of mine has a disastrous burden on her heart, and I greatly fear, Hamilton, she cherishes the wild purpose of making you her father confessor."

"Oh! no, uncle, the tragic element would vanish on the mortal spot if I changed my attitude from that of patience on a monument smiling at grief."[34]

"I'm afraid you wouldn't be capable of anything more serious than a smile if grief did come near you," said Hamilton, with his steady pleasant gaze.

Hamilton looked his age; thirty-three. He was tall and thin, slightly stooped from constant desk work, and wore that pale and grave air of the hard student. His eyes were long and brown, but their gaze denoted near-sightedness, his complexion was as clear and as fair as a girl's, only a little pallid for the want of sunshine, perhaps. His brown hair was thin and silky and he wore a long brown moustache. His face was not handsome, but was full of thoughtful, scholarly refinement. His long white neck and slender white hands, the right one cramped from much writing, spoke too strongly of delicacy, but lent a not unpleasant interest to the

---

34. Viola, referring to her own unrequited love in Shakespeare's *Twelfth Night*.

man. He was an ardent student and writer in a field that means much labour and small remuneration—exclusively devoted to Irish subjects; and was at present engaged in a "History of the Rebellions" which had waved over the political ocean of Ireland.

The subject had been done before, of course; but, probably, he entertained the hope of doing it better than it had yet been done. He had already published a book of Irish translations, chiefly songs and legends, and some papers, really abstruse, on Irish archaeology, all of which proved him a learned Irish scholar. But his talents were of a versatile order. He had acquired a deep knowledge of European politics about which he wrote much, and there was scarcely a Continental literature and language with which he was not intimately acquainted.

He had independent means—inherited from his father—as well as what he earned by his pen. Marjory always spoke of him as "the eligible," and wondered how it was that he and Morna were not engaged, considering he seemed to be very earnestly in love, and Morna certainly showed a preference for his society.

Though I am not prepared to state that his life in the past had precisely resembled that of an anchorite, I can safely announce that he was no rake, and had sufficient modesty to regard the woman he loved as immeasurably too good for him.

"Did you accomplish anything remarkable down in the office today?" he asked of Marjory, with a gravity that might easily be construed into a sneer.

"No; I've never tried to do anything since I moved a resolution that the Central Executive should hold a meeting to discuss the probability of the Chief using whitewash for blacking in cleaning his boots in Kilmainham, and to propose a vote of five shillings a week to Mr. John Francis Davoren for curl papers and cosmetics. Oh, yes, I moved at Christmas that a manifesto should be sent out in my name urging all over the country an increase of drums and banners at the local meetings, and I entertained some thoughts of proposing a National Convention of ladies to be held in the

Rotunda while the men are in prison."

"And what did *la grande Mademoiselle* say to this very admirable proposition?" asked Hamilton, gravely.

"Looked at me for five minutes as if she believed me actually capable of getting the announcement surreptitiously printed and flinging it broadcast on the country. Then she changed her mind and laughed. She regarded me as hopelessly frothy, you know."

"I'd like to know how, in the name of goodness, she could possibly regard you as anything else," laughed her uncle.

"Your sister is in, is she not?" asked Hamilton, in suppressed eagerness.

As she asked the question the door opened and admitted Morna, followed by Power. She smiled almost warmly as she shook hands with Hamilton, but he did not smile; his face seemed bathed in a deep, grave light. His look of happiness was only marred by the touch of anxiety in his voice, as he said:

"I greatly feared you had returned to the office."

"No, I promised Marjory to devote some time to the entertainment of you and Mr. Power first."

"I am rejoiced that our claims are to be remembered, even through the affairs of State," said Power, loftily. "Marjory, have you yet discovered how that man did not know that it was my Lord Silchester?"[35]

"Never. It is very strange, Mark, he did not know it was my Lord Silchester."

"Don't you think it would be only fair to make me a sharer of the joke?" asked Hamilton, seeing every one laughed immoderately.

"What! You haven't heard the story of my Lord Silchester? Nay, then, you are indeed, unblest," cried Marjory solemnly. "Last summer we were lodging out in Marley, and our landlady was a very imposing person, indeed. She always wore a lace cap with pink

---

35. Lord Silchester and Lord Granby: possibly anecdotal. The Silchester title is associated with the Earls of Longford (thePeerage.com). Lynch published a story in 1897, 'A Village Sovereign', that features a Marquess of Grandby.

roses in it, and a silk apron. She was quite remarkable – dropped her h's, spoke pathetically of her dear dead 'usband's hestate down in 'Ackney, was, in fact, an English hofficer's wife. One day two gentlemen arrived post haste from Dublin, and handed her a letter. She opened it, and found it was from a colonel's wife, whom she had known in India, recommending to her care her friends, Lord Silchester and Lord Granby, who wanted rooms in Marley, and would, she felt sure, be charmingly accommodated at her friend's house. When she read the letter, a thrill ran through her being. She rose, looked on the noble lords who were sitting in well-bred composure, with their aristocratic birth and titles written in visible letters on their faces; rose and made that low curtsey generally believed to belong to the time of Queen Anne, and with her head nearly on a level with their varnished boots, said:

"Your lordships are most welcome to my 'umble dwelling. What would your noble lordships be pleased to require?"

Picture the face of the noble lords on the occasion! The rooms were small, but the noble lords were pleased to express themselves as highly delighted with everything they saw, and took their departure, announcing the fact that their valets—she didn't believe in the French language and preferred to give every letter its full value—would come later on with their luggage. The valets came, but mark! the noble lords gave a gentle single tap like beggarmen, but the common valets thundered as if they thought themselves the noble lords, turned up their noses at the rooms, which they described as mere rat-holes, and, on the whole, acted in striking contrast with the behaviour of the noble lords. "The next day my Lord Granby went away, placing in my hand a ten-pound note," said Mrs. Greely. So like a noble lord! It's my opinion my Lord Granby had enough of the place after one night. The next day my Lord Silchester dined in the Shelbourne, and after dinner he went for a walk and found himself somewhere in the neighbourhood of Ballsbridge, when he discovered that two of the waiters of the hotel had followed him to waylay him and steal his money and valuables. There was a scuffle, and my Lord Silchester was flung into a ditch with a bruised head. There he lay till a man passed by, and looking down into the ditch, cried out: 'Halloa, Chappy!' He did not know it was my Lord Silchester. Mark! he did not know.

"'Take me to the house of the good Mrs. Greely,' cried the noble lord, piteously."

"That observation of the noble lord is remarkably suggestive of our early French exercise books," smiled Power.

"It was a very singular fact that this ordinary labourer knew the good Mrs. Greely quite well," Marjory went on, in her assumed solemn air. "My lord was conveyed to his room without meeting Mrs. Greely, and he sent for her. 'I went upstairs,' said Mrs. Greely, 'and lo! I found the noble lord sitting with his head bent over his hand, and lying back in an arm-chair. I could not think what had happened to his lordship, and advanced on tip-toe. "I trust your lordship's mother is well," I asked, quite frightened. "I've been *bet*," said my Lord Silchester, raising his bruised forehead, "I'm dead bet," (fancy a Peer of England saying 'I've been *bet*'). 'I at once applied a raw beefsteak to his noble brow, which I touched reverentially. In a few days he was quite well, and he handed me twenty-five pounds, saying, "Irishmen broke my head, but Irish women mended it."'"

Hamilton laughed unrestrainedly. In any case the mere fact that Morna, enjoyed the story so thoroughly would have been quite sufficient to make it amusing to him. But the originality of Marjory's looks and gestures was such to give a special colour to each word she uttered perfectly untransmissible on paper. Her attitude and voice and look, when she imitated the noble lord shielding his wounded brow with his hand, and then looking up and saying, "I've been *bet*," was an admirable piece of humorous acting, and shook both Power and Morna in a thrill of silent laughter.

"Was there ever such a girl?" asked Power, throwing back his head and gazing meditatively at the ceiling.

"Fine frescoes, those," said Marjory, in demure gravity, as she pointed to the ordinary whitewashed ceiling.

Power laughed good-humouredly.

"You and I come off just as badly as my Lord Silchester at this young lady's hands when we are absent, Power," said Hamilton, moving his chair a little away from the tea-table and leaning against it sideways.

"Mr. Power may, but you know I'm hopelessly in love with you, Mr. Hamilton."

"Indeed, I know no such thing, Miss Marjory," rejoined Hamilton, looking at Morna.

"He means that it isn't hopeless," said Power, relishing the inaccuracy of the inference.

"Ah, it's too late now; you wouldn't have me when you might, and I had to solace myself with another."

"I must say you seem pretty well consoled, but then a lawn-tennis young man is capable of making up a great deal of bereavement," sneered Hamilton.

"Why not? I went to see some suspects in Galway, and the Captain—Golding, I think—having walked into the room, 'Do you play tennis? He asked, pronouncing it 'tenise.' When I said 'No,' he urged, insinuatingly, 'Ah, now, I'm sure you play tennis; I know by your face you do.' When the captain of one of her Majesty's prisons plays tennis, why shouldn't Frank Harston?" she retorted.

"Are you going back to the office this evening?" asked Hamilton in a lower tone, as he turned to Morna, who had risen from the tea-table.

"Yes, I think I'll go now. You are in very good company with Marjory, and can spare me," she said, with unconscious coquetry.

"You don't believe that, Miss Maurice," he answered, gravely. "Will you let me walk across town with you? I have much to say to you. I have been greatly troubled by some things that have been circulated about me, and, though I have deferred pressing for another kind of claim, owing to the fact that you are working very hard now, and are too much worried with office troubles and all that, I still hold to my claims on you as a friend. It may be that you will refuse to let me be more to you, however earnestly and ardently I hope for the blessing, yet I know, Morna, you will never ask me to be less. You will let me walk with you to Sackville-street, won't you?"36

"Yes, yes. I'm sorry, oh, I'm deeply sorry to know that you're in trouble. Have I shown a disposition to forget the claims of friendship ever? I hoped it was not so. I don't know how it will end for you or me, or any of us. But, trust me, whatever happens it will be for the best. You know everything belonging to my own personal life is remote from me now. I have no time to think of my own life now, and the snatches of indolence I have are devoted to rest and to thinking of Marjory. But I'll go now if you like. My things are downstairs."

"Going so soon, Miss Morna?" cried Power.

"You're going across with her, Hamilton?" said Mr. Maurice.

(To be Continued – Commenced in No. 949.)

Vol. XXII. – No. 954.
Saturday, January 24, 1885: 261–263.

CHAPTER IX

THE WALK TO THE OFFICE.

"What has troubled you, Mr. Hamilton?" asked Morna, looking back from the step as Hamilton closed the door.

The night was clear and starlit, and the dark foliage of the Green seemed to reach the sky itself, against which it made a thick mass of intense black, relieved by the darkling glitter of the stars.

---

36. The Ladies' Land League was established by Anna Parnell at a meeting held at 39 Upper Sackville Street, Dublin, 31 January 1881.

"You will, perhaps, blame me for minding what people say of me," answered Hamilton, looking down as he walked beside her, sometimes beating the pavement with his stick. "I know it is absurd, but it has worried me."

"Well, candidly, I do blame you. Why should trivialities worry you, above all reports that haven't a ground of truth in them? Read the things that are been constantly written of us on the Conservative papers, and by the English Press, too. And yet we only laugh at them. Didn't some English comic paper show us up drinking brandy, smoking cigars with our feet on tables, and pistols sticking out of our jackets. Could anything be worse than that? And yet we didn't worry ourselves."[37]

"Yes, yes, I know. But those were said by enemies. Nothing is considered too brutal in party strife. I wouldn't mind if the *Express* described me as a Moonlighter or anything else; but I'm referring to things that have been said of me by our own friends."[38]

"Oh, of course, that is painful; but you can't hope to escape it. We have been pained in the same way. Our own party are scarcely kinder to us than our enemies. They don't exactly look on us in the same light as the *Express;* but if I had to make a choice between the brutalities of our enemies or the passive dislike of our male friends, I candidly confess I'd prefer the former."

"God bless me! Do you say so, Miss Maurice? Are you referring to the men in prison?" asked Hamilton, in surprise.

"Well, I don't want you to think I refer to them in particular. I am sometimes inclined to believe that it is the real *raison d'être* of women to be worried and pained by men."

---

37. A reference to the numerous satiric depictions and lampoons of the Ladies' Land League appearing in the press, including various cartoons in *Funny Folks*.
38. Moonlighter: one of a group of people who perpetrated night raids on tenants believed to oppose the Land League. "moonlighter, n.". *OED Online*. Oxford University Press. https://www-oed-com.

"Oh! don't say that, please, don't, Morna," urged her companion, looking round into her face with his earnest, softened glance. "You will make me feel that I am adding to your worry, and I wouldn't. God knows there is no trouble I wouldn't gladly bear for your sake. There, do not mind what I said coming out. It doesn't matter. But promise me you will not believe I wanted to worry or pain you."

"Now you will make me feel that you are not really the friend you say when you are so ready to take up seriously every irritable word of mine. If I have seen a great deal of how men persecute women in domestic life and crush out their individuality and moral strength I am none the less disposed to believe in the thorough goodness of a man like you when I meet him. The system men pursue in private they would most certainly pursue in public life if it should unfortunately come to pass that women generally entered public careers. I believe, whatever our friends or enemies may think to the contrary, that the Ladies' Land League is doing good and useful work. We work hard, all of us, and I plainly believe the organisation would have fallen through at the time of the general imprisonment of the members if our body hadn't been in existence. It is quite probable they'll now refuse to admit that to you, but at least we have the country's testimony that we are prompt correspondents. I sometimes wish Forster[39] would put us all in prison to and make an end of us, or that Mr. Parnell would relieve us from our post by dissolving us.[40] A dissolution was proposed among ourselves, but we recognised that it would be dishonourable and cowardly to run away until we had officially learned that our services were no longer required. Mr. Hamilton, I hope there will never be another

---

39. W. E. Forster (1818–1886): Chief Secretary for Ireland (1880–1882), strongly opposed to the Land League and its activities. https://www.dib.ie/biography/forster-william-edward-a3334
40. The dissolution of the Ladies' Land League was finalised in August 1882. See Anna Parnell's depiction of the dissolution in *The Tale of a Great Sham*, (in Hearne, ed. 2020, pp. 149–158). See also Dana Hearne's detailed discussion of the complexities of this dissolution which Lynch's narrative illustrates (2020, pp. xlvi-liii).

Ladies' Land League. And now pray tell me about yourself. Who has been saying unkind things of you?"

"Well, you perfectly understand why I never became more than a mere member of the Land League, don't you?"

"Certainly; you have a great deal of other work to do, and, considering you are working for Irish literature, your patriotism is just as exalted as if you were addressing meetings from morning till night, and forming branches of the Land League between the pauses," said Morna, laughing.

"Well, I have often been tempted to question my right to content myself with giving an annual subscription, and attending meetings whenever I found leisure to do so," he returned doubtfully. "It had occurred to me more than once that I should not give up my time so exclusively to private work when the country is so disturbed, and that I had the right to throw myself into the battle."

"Well, yes," said Morna, slowly.

"You think so?" he questioned eagerly.

"I will confess to you that I have wondered why you were satisfied to remain a spectator," said Morna.

"There it is, you didn't say that to me before, and I felt I was wrong."

"Pray, don't mistake me; I do not wish you to believe that I think you were wrong in not becoming more prominent; I only said I wondered at you for not doing so, considering your high and disinterested patriotism. I think men of your stamp are necessary to every movement which is born of high purpose. The Land League is too widespread for us to believe that all its members are purely patriotic. You are of the Robert Emmet[41] type—the type which fashioned the leaders of the '48 movement."

Hamilton's pallid face flushed with candid delight.

---

41. Robert Emmet (1778–1803): Irish nationalist, patriot and United Irishman. His involvement in a failed rebellion resulted in a trial and his famous speech from the dock, followed by his execution. Patrick M. Geoghegan, 'Robert Emmet', *DIB*, https://www.dib.ie/biography/emmet-robert-a2921

"No praise in the world could ever be so sweet to me as yours. If you think so well of me, why—why do you think so lightly of my love?"

"I don't think lightly of it. I value it as a tribute of singular worth and beauty. I can't tell you how proud I am that a devotion so high and worthy as yours should be offered to me. I have seen too much of the worthlessness of men's love for women not to rate yours as a beautiful blessing, if—if I could accept it," she said, gravely.

"And why not?"

There was so much encouragement in her grave words that he stopped suddenly, laid his hand on her arm, and urged more rapidly:

"With me your life will be precisely as it has hitherto been. Your poor will become my poor—your charities I will share. Your political work will continue as now until circumstances will have released you, and then, Morna, think how much marriage—a marriage such as ours will be—broadens and completes a woman's life. All the sweetest duties of womanhood come through marriage. Whose nature can be so full, so perfect, as that of a wife and a mother? And, Morna, you are a very ideal of perfect womanhood. Think how lonely you will be when this agitation is over and Marjory is married. Say you will have me then."

"How can I? You think too highly of me, I fear. I have no disbelief in the beauty of perfect marriage. But when I look round I think it must be an ideal only, for I see nothing to justify our hope in it. You are good and true, and I know if there were any man noble and large-hearted enough not to seek to narrow my sympathies with others, and to restrict me in the circle of duties I have made for myself outside home, that man would be you assuredly. But I don't think I am made for love of that sort. I don't know how to make you understand. If I could feel it I should feel it for you. You believe me! Pray do. But I feel I couldn't abandon even for you my grand ideal of what my own life shall be. I don't think marriage broadens the sympathies; it restricts them to the home circle. A father and mother are only the father and mothers of their own children. I would like to take the children of the universe into my arms. I never see a ragged, unwashed little child in the street without wishing to take it home with me. I think I could be more useful in the world unmarried. Until I joined the Ladies' Land League I had a great deal more to do than would be possible for me to do even as your wife. And then there is another thing I wonder if I can make you understand, because men find it hard, I know, to believe such things of women," she added, in a lower tone, looking straight before her, her firm, pale face outlined sharply in the dim light and the self-sustained poise of her shapely head deepening the maidenly pride of her words. "It has always been my ideal to fashion my life on lines as clear as those of Hypatia."[42]

"Do you mean you will enter a convent?" asked Hamilton, in startled sadness.

"No, not that. I cling to the warmth of home and home affections. I love to come home from the sorrows and soreness of the outer world to my uncle, with his cheery ways, back to Marjory's indestructible brightness and happy laughter. Then, too, I would miss my independence, my books, my friendships, and all the pleasant items of my life, which do not prevent it from resembling otherwise what it might be in a convent."

"No, no; it is a thousand times lovelier as it is. You understand, I worship you. I will always do so, whether you remain my white, distant Hypatia, diffusing holiness and love around you, or become my visible home Madonna, bringing me the precious sweetness of a close and unalterable love all my own. Give me leave to speak to

---

42. Hypatia: (c. 370–415), Greek philosopher, astronomer, and mathematician. Head of the Neoplatonist school at Alexandria, she wrote several learned treatises as well as devising inventions such as an astrolabe. ("Hypatia". *Oxford Reference*. https://www.oxfordreference.com/view/10.1093/oi/authority.20110810105119416.). A remarkable woman who offered a model of female independence and scholarship, representing alternatives to marriage in Lynch's tale.

you of this once again, when your work here is over."

They were now at the office. She looked at him with her grave eyes, grey eyes, and smiled a warm, soft smile.

"I will, but I think my answer will be the same. And about yourself?"

"Oh, I'll take your advice. They were right in assuming that I'm a coward because I'm not in prison. I've never made a speech, but to-morrow I'll address a meeting somewhere. You'll come to see me in prison?".

CHAPTER X

A DELICATE CONVERSATION.

In a warmly-lighted smoking-room in a manorial Meath establishment known to belong to the Nevilles—a highly respectable family, branching prolifically through the country—sat two young gentlemen smoking, and drinking brandy and soda-water through the pauses of conversation.

"Why did you send that letter saying you'd go up to town to-morrow?" Asked the elder of the two, a largely-built, swarthy individual, with a face lined heavily with years of dissipation.

"Oh, because I thought it just as well to get the thing over at once," returned his companion, on whose unindividualistic face dissipation was beginning to draw its incipient lines; his figure inclined to heaviness, and in his well-cut features was gathered a promising amount of cruelty, weakness, and selfish indolence.

"So you've quite made up your mind to go in for the Trediger girl?"

"Quite. Where's the use of asking that question?" was the moody reply.

"Nothing more reasonable, Frank. I mean to have a dash with this little one myself, now that you cry off."

"Neville, do you want me to knock you down?"

"That's a feat beyond your fist. But why shouldn't I? I'm hard hit on those golden curls of hers already. You'd better send me on your message and remain where you are. You had, really."

"No, I won't."

"But haven't you ceased to care a hang about her?" urged his friend.

"Who the devil ever said I had? I was hard hit about her enough, but she's the damnedest little flirt alive."

"Precisely. Then why shouldn't she flirt with me as well as another fellow? You can't prevent her, and you're only acting the part of the dog in the manger now since you're going to give her up."

Frank Harston only grunted and buried his face in his tumbler.

"No—it's a deuced hard thing to do well, I know," he said, putting aside his tumbler and puffing reflectively.

"Most things are deucedly hard, you know," rejoined his friend, in cheerful assent.

"No, they are not. It wouldn't be hard to go back and make love hard and fast to Marjory. I tell you what it is Joe, I'd enjoy nothing better."

"Yes, you would. You'd enjoy the Tredigers' money in the long run much better. Take my word for it, money wears better than love," said his philosophic comrade.

"Yes, and you're sure about the fortune, Joe? Fifteen thousand?"

"Not a shadow of a doubt of it."

"Fifteen thousand is a big sum. I question if Marjory's uncle would give her five hundred."

"He might and he mightn't. It's generally well to be sure. Looking at it from the most hopeful point of view it would still be fourteen thousand five hundred less than the Trediger would bring you."

Frank gasped a little. The difference sounded enormous.

"But Marjory is so infernally pretty, and though she has joined that abominable Land League, she is a lady to the tips of her fingers, and by jove she's devilish fond of me I can tell you. If you saw her in evening dress you'd be awfully proud of her, Joe, and she's such good value. But the other"—

"Stuff and nonsense. Louisa Trediger is a splendid girl, tip-top figure, a little heavy, like your own, my dear fellow. She is not, perhaps, refined at present, but she'll tone down under your care, and then, you know, she's a magnificent hand at tennis."

"Yes; that is a consideration," said Frank gravely, with all the air of a man who had reached the finest and strongest point of his case. A fortuneless wife is an evil a young gentleman would naturally be expected to shrink from, but a wife who does not play tennis could not but rest as a heavy stumbling-block to the happiness and exalted aspirations of a young gentleman proficient in that intellectual art. Marjory did not play tennis and Louisa Trediger did; furthermore, Marjory was gilded with a too-problematical five hundred, and Louisa Trediger shone through the golden sum of fifteen thousand. Naturally his reason and intellect, or whatever stood him in its stead, urged him to the feet of Miss Trediger.

"I wonder what stuff is in the uncle," he observed after a long pause.

"What uncle? Little Marjory's?" asked Neville, reaching for another cigar.

"Yes, you met him at the Hammam."[43]

"Oh, I remember, the fellow with the large feet encased in square tops—a trader, or something like that!"

Frank Harston nodded. His vanity was severely wounded by his friend's tone.

---

43. Hammam: Turkish baths in Dublin feature most famously in James Joyce's *Ulysses*. The brief reference to a meeting here, implying social status or lack of, could be to the Hammam Family hotel and Turkish Baths, O'Connell Street (established in 1869), the Leinster St. Turkish and Warm Baths or the Lincoln Place baths. See for further details on their social significance in the period: Teresa Breathnach, 'For Health and Pleasure: The Turkish Bath in Victorian Ireland". *Victorian Literature and Culture*, vol. 32, no. 1, 2004, pp. 159–175.

"You're afraid he may be in the habit of carrying a pistol or a horse-whip under his coat-tails?" laughed Neville.

"I didn't mean that," said Frank, sulkily.

"Then what in the name of goodness are you afraid of? An action?"

Harston flushed deeply.

"Oh, no. The Maurices are a cut above that," he eagerly interposed.

"Oh, then settle the matter at once if you care about my opinion. Write the girl a letter, and say that cruel circumstances, over which will and heart have unfortunately no control, prevent your aspiring to the honour of an alliance with her, that the honour would be, in fact, greater than you could bear in your present circumstances, &c., &c. If you like I'll add a postscript saying that you are held down quite helpless by two ruffians of uncles, five waspish maiden aunts, and twelve first cousins, to say nothing of a host of second and third."

Harston laughed in spite of his uneasiness, and drank more brandy.

"I couldn't for the life of me write that letter. It would make her cry, and I'd be miserable. I'd prefer to get out of the matter more quietly."

"Well, if there is any honour in the whole thing that would certainly be the most honourable way. It is cowardly to shrink out of the thing, and you know you mean to make her cry in any case."

"Yes, but don't you see it would be far pleasanter to tell her while I'm making love to her, that I am forced by brutal circumstances to postpone anything like a definite engagement till I feel surer of getting my profession. I can pretend the governor has stopped my allowance. Then by degrees I'll cease writing to her, and she'll know nothing more till I'm Louisa Trediger's husband."

Neville sipped his brandy and soda, and gazed gravely into the fire. He understood his friend's dilemma, and appreciated the reasons which made him hesitate to carry out a former promise with such a brilliant matrimonial chance in view, but he did not quite approve of his method of conveying his withdrawal to that pretty little witch up in Dublin.

"You'd better let me go, Frank. I might fall in love with the little one and console her for her loss," he urged again.

"Do you want me to knock you down?" asked Harston with a slightly incoherent utterance. "Damn it! I'm fond of her."

"Well, you were fond of others, too, and got over it. Weren't you hard hit on Evelyn Handcock and on Tiny Humphreys?"

"By George! I was. Do you remember Tiny? I don't think I ever saw a pair of eyes as black as Tiny's. Wasn't I going to cut my throat about her once? But I'll see Marjory."

CHAPTER XI

A CHANCE MEETING.

Marjory was in the office when Frank Harston called at Leeson-street. He drove there at once and left word with a messenger he met in the hall that he was on his way to the Jesuits' House, and would return for young Miss Maurice shortly.

"There, Marjory, is Froth," cried a lively lady Land Leaguer, who was watching Harston jump up on an outside car. "I declare he's such an inveterate flirt that he is actually attitudinising before the carman. Look at him lying back."

"That is not a very complimentary way to talk of Romeo to Juliet," said Marjory, with a short excited laugh as she approached the window and looked out. "But if you call him Froth, he is just as uncomplimentary to you; he calls you 'the Frothy Executive.'"

"Why? When pray did he see us?"

"Oh, he took great stock of you all at the Convention."

Marjory's business capacities, such as they were, were very

seriously impaired by that transient vision of her lover; her brow, eye, lips, and cheeks flashed in an electrical wave of light; and when he returned from a momentous visit to Father Trediger, the uncle of the lady of lawn-tennis notoriety, he found her in the radiance of happy expectant girlhood.

"Frank, you heartless old fiend, why didn't you keep your promise and come up on Friday?" she asked, nestling towards him for an instant when they were alone, and pressing a fluttering butterfly kiss on his shoulder, which was nearest her lips.

"Oh, come now, Marjory, you're not going to scold a fellow surely. 'Pon my soul, darling, I was mad to be up with you, but, you understand, Neville is such a confounded queer fellow; one has to humour him, or he's sure to play the devil with a fellow's nerves. Is Morna inside?"

"Yes; she is very busy. Wait and see her in Leeson-street this evening."

They talked over the accustomed ground during their walk. It is problematical how Adam and Eve made love, but most lovers downwards have shown a remarkable absence of originality in the process. Yet I doubt if many girls are as radiantly spontaneous and merry as Marjory was. At the Green Harston proposed a short adjournment for rest and seclusion; he was devilishly worried, he said, and had a lot of things to explain to her.

They sat opposite the lake, heedless of the swans and brown ducks. Harston's glances were ardent enough, protectively-appealing and self-deploring; could they be otherwise with a summer bird of shining eyes and plumage and full-throated laughter beside him, and the knowledge that what had so lately been an eager delight in his life was now about to be abandoned! It is so deuced hard on a susceptible fellow like him.

"I'm in awful trouble, Marge," he broke out, shaking his head despondently.

"No! how so, Frank?" Marjory gasped.

"That governor of mine has fixed on me devilishly badly. He

talks of stopping my allowance, Marge, and he means it, too."

"You haven't been quarrelling, have you?"

"Oh, not quite; that is, there is some girl—a horrible fright I loathe—down in Wicklow he wants me to marry, and because I won't he threatens to stop my allowance. I wouldn't care a hang if I were earning an income and were able to marry you at once."

"Oh, Frank, will I be the cause of your starving or having a lot of trouble?"

"It looks deuced like it," he said, shaking his head slowly, and then drawing her hand within his arm and pressing it reassuringly; "but what does it matter so long as I have you, darling?"

She was vaguely troubled as he meant she should be—a breath of wind from the far-off sorrow that was awaiting her—why should this father start up so unaccountably between them? What were their lives to his that he should seek to asunder them? Frank had not been influenced by his father in making his engagement, then why should be influenced by him in breaking it off? Why, what nonsense her mind was wandering into? Who had spoken of breaking off? Not her own foolish old Frank. Then why should she? Others had begun wedded life in poverty and had struggled very happily through adverse times. If Frank was strong enough for it, she was stronger still.

"We can wait, Marge," he said, looking into her troubled eyes and poor white face. "Eventually everything must be mine."

She shivered a little, and tried to laugh off the weight that oppressed her, but sorrow had vaguely stirred the glad depths of her eyes and blasted the happy light of her face.

She rose and approached the water-edge. Standing there she saw Denzil Dalrymple and Brecknock crossing the bridge. They saluted her from the distance and hastened towards her.

"Who are those fellows grinning like idiots?" asked Harston, rising and approaching her.

"Friends of Evelyn Handcock's—naval officers."

"I'm so glad to meet you again, Miss Maurice," said Denzil,

sincerely. "I was wondering if I'd ever have the chance of asking permission to call on you and your sister."

"Morna will be glad to see you," said Marjory, gravely. "Permit me to introduce you to my friend, Mr. Harston."

Denzil remembered the name and a certain relationship, and bowed civilly; Brecknock stared at him a little impertinently, and turned to Marjory with a gaze of slow admiration.

"Of course, I claim the permission accorded my friend; I may call, too."

(To be Continued – Commenced in No. 949.)

Vol. XXII. – No. 955.
Saturday, January 31, 1885: 275–277.

CHAPTER XII

BRECKNOCK AND DALRYMPLE VISIT AT LEESON-STREET.

During the walk home Frank was naturally sulky; this meeting with unknown naval officers, one of them so confoundedly handsome, too, was a reasonable ground for offence. Marjory was pathetic in her efforts at gaiety, then her mood changed, and she, too, became—shall we acknowledge it?—just a little cross. It is all very well to throw a girl over when you suppose you are leaving her to forlornness and heartache, but, by Jove, it is quite another thing when two naval officers start suddenly on the scene. No fellow likes that, and really it is an injustice when you look at it in the right way. We are Turks, sir, all of us, and we like to hold the making or marring of a woman's life in our own hands. And why not, pray? This little thing by his side now, could he not make her laugh, or smile, or weep at will? Then what the devil right had a handsome officer to want to call on her?

"Won't you come in, Frank?" she asked at the door, with eyes that spoke far more than her words; appeal seemed to tremble on her eyelashes, and the mouth, till now a red negation of sorrow, was a crimson droop of pain.

"I don't know that I ought to," he said, stiffening his head and neck in sulky coldness. "I can't understand a girl picking up with a pair of idiots with such alacrity."

"Frank, why will you be so jealous? Can't you understand that I do not only love you, I adore you?" she cried, passionately.

Well, the sulkiest young man ought to be capable of being mollified by such a soothing assertion. Of course he went in and was as ardent and demonstrative as needs be; brave, too, if bravery consists in a protested capacity for facing a dozen angry fathers, for conquering universes by the overmastering strength of his love, &c. He even shed some tears—none of your French heroic tears, please, but real genuine manly Irish tears; tears not of maudlin sentiment, but from the depth of his soul; thought that he and Marjory revived the old passion of Romeo and Juliet, and swore that Marjory in that character was worth all your Ellen Terrys and Modjeskas.[44] She was, if truth is worth fiction, but Juliet herself at no time felt more sadly prophetic than she when her lover left her, to watch the firelight and muse while waiting for Morna.

"Had you a happy day with Frank?" asked Morna, coming behind her and drawing her face up to kiss the bit of white forehead under the fluffy, bright hair.

"Yes, yes. We met Mr. Brecknock and his handsome friend. They stopped and asked if they might call on us. Of course, I said yes."

"Indeed," said Morna, with a surprised look.

---

44. Famous actresses of the period, Ellen Terry (1847–1928), popular English actress celebrated for diverse performances and dramatic partnerships and Helena Modjeska (1840–1909), Polish-American actress especially known for her Shakespearean performances.

"Morna, I am very low-spirited this evening. Frank and I had a tiff, and I suppose I haven't got rid of its effects on me yet. I'm wondering if I'll ever again be so wildly, so exuberantly happy as I was last summer. Do you remember the days of the Convention?"[45]

"What makes you adopt that gloomy strain of 'do you remember,' child?"

"Nothing. I've just been going back over my whole life, and I know what would be my answer if I were asked, like Napoleon, which was the happiest day of my life."

"Of course you do. The day Frank told you he loved you."

"No, Morna, it wasn't. It was the day of the Convention last September. That was the most beautiful, the brightest day within my memory. The enthusiasm of it, the wild excitement, the wonderful grandeur of the whole thing! Oh, I can understand the passionate madness of a people for its king, and the chief is our uncrowned king. He always reminds me of these lines:

'Hail to the chief who in triumph advances!

Honour'd and bless'd be the ever-green pine.'[46]

But what connection he can have in my mind with pine I don't know," she broke off with a sudden little laugh, staying the mournfulness of voice and look.

Morna looked at her several times in puzzled wonder. Why had she been talking that way about the Convention as past happiness, and now in her uncle's presence gushing in frantic, feverish, mirth—through anecdote and simile, mimicking Frank, Brecknock, and Denzil, and everybody? And yet so charming through all. Morna thought of Browning's beautiful lines:

"O, Lyric love, half angel and half bird,
And all a wonder and a wild desire."[47]

---

45. The Land League Convention opened with a speech by Charles Parnell on the 15th September 1881.
46. The opening lines of Sir Walter Scott's 'The Lady of the Lake: Boat Song' (1810).
47. Lines from Browning's 'The Ring and the Book' (1869–9).

What, in heaven's name, could Harston have been quarrelling with her about?

"I've a good mind to say to you what we used to say to the children long ago, Marge," cried her uncle, drying his eyes, moist with laughter: "so much laughing will end in crying by night."

What was it made Morna fancy the laughter was so perilously near trembling off into tears? Ah, well, it was probably some love trouble that a week's sulk and worry would heal.

"Don't go back to the office to-night, Morna."

"I must; you know how much I have to do, my pet. But I wish I could stay with you," said Morna, kissing her eyelids. "I hear there is a warrant out for Herbert Hamilton. You read his speech yesterday."

"I hope they'll send him to Kilmainham, and I'll go to see him," said Marjory.

The next morning Morna received a telegram from Hamilton, telling of his arrest and imprisonment in Kilmainham; he would expect her soon.

"Poor fellow! I wish he had loved my little Marjory and she had chosen him instead of that frivolous popinjay," she sighed.

This was Tuesday. On Wednesday Denzil and Brecknock called. Morna was never seen in Leeson-street between breakfast and dinner in the evening. But on this day she was tortured with a headache, and came home at one o'clock in the hope of getting rid of it by rest and silence.

Marjory was sitting on the hearthrug, reading by firelight, with bent head and flushed cheeks, while Morna lay in an arm-chair with closed eyes and her feet on the fender, when the young men were announced and at once shown in. Marjory was warm and glowing, and looked more like a dainty porcelain statue, thrilled with its minute life, than the delicate white flower she usually looked. Brecknock thought Evelyn Handcock coarse and noisy beside her, and felt half in love with her already. Morna lifted up her head with white cheeks and languid eyes.

"I owe my sister's presence here to what I should call an

unfortunate chance," said Marjory, shaking hands with them. "She has managed to knock herself up quite, and has come home to me to be nursed and petted and made much of."

"It's rather worth one's while getting knocked up for such charming results," drawled Brecknock, while Denzil leant forward towards Morna, with his grave glance, and said:

"You do look tired and ill, Miss Maurice. Is it quite necessary that patriotism should test your powers so far?"

"It shouldn't by right. It only proves my own weakness. But it is nothing more than a bad headache. Have you seen Miss Handcock lately?"

Something like a flush waved over Denzil's face, as he remembered Evelyn's last conversation with him and its painful results for himself.

"Yes. Do you like Miss Handcock?" he asked boldly.

Morna answered his question with a gravely surprised look.

"She is a very good-natured girl, far better than she imagines herself to be. We were school-fellows, and I like her sincerely, but we differ in nearly all our opinions."

"Yes, I know; politics, for instance."

"Well, put it that way if you like," she said, smiling, "but really you do Evelyn an injustice. I don't think she knows anything about politics, and only troubles herself so far as believing that everything Conservative must necessarily be perfect."

"She calls the Conservatives dear, sweet, and amiable, sometimes even too perfectly distracting," said Marjory with her serious air. "The Liberals are just tolerable; I think she has even found a Liberal quite too charming, but that is an exceptionable experience, I assure you. As for Radicals or Nationalists, they are supremely, unutterably odious—degradation itself."

"Marge, Marge," remonstrated Morna, as the visitors joined in hearty laughter.

Denzil contrasted Miss Maurice's way of discussing her friend with that of the young lady of his order, and was struck with the large-mindedness and generosity of the former. Yes, he did well in coming and judging the girl for himself before condemning her even for such breaches of propriety and womanliness as midnight drives unescorted on outside cars. Her eyes were nothing less wonderful, and her look and manner the more attractive for a slight languor and weariness.

Two days afterwards he was seriously deliberating within himself what excuse he could invent for another visit to Leeson-street, when Brecknock lounged into his room, tugging at his beard with one hand and twirling his watch-guard with the other.

"Say, Den, suppose we call on those girls, the Land Leaguers? I'm deuced hit on that little one, I am. Gad, Den, she's fetching, she is; and I've half a mind to throw over Evy and go in for her hard and fast. You know I'm a bit of a socialist, after my fashion, and there's no one but that brother of mine to kick up a row, and, by Jove, if the little one has me, he may blaze away to the devil if he likes."

"You're a large-minded fellow, no doubt," said Denzel, with a curious thrill that sent his pulses beating faster. It seemed odd, no doubt, that his companion's thoughts should be drifting towards the same channel as his own; and Brecknock's prejudices ought to be more difficult to overcome, seeing he was the scion of a magnificent old Welsh stock. "But you seem to have given no thought to the fact that the girl is already engaged."

"Oh, that's only Evy Handcock's talk. I've no doubt that chap we met in the Green the other day—by Jove, his dress showed some taste, I can tell you; I wonder, now, is his tailor Irish; not that fellow I was sent to, I'm certain, for he's an abominable slow cut, he is. Didn't I show you that beastly tweed suit he sent me home, with one of your big West End prices, too, nailed on to it! Yes, I've no doubt he is spooney on her, there's nothing wonderful in that. Don't you think, Den, Arthur Brecknock of Brecknock Manor runs a fair chance of cutting out a Dublin masher?"[48]

---

48. An American term for a womaniser.

Denzil laughed and looked thoughtfully at the end of his cigar. It would clearly suit his purpose to bring Brecknock up with the hope of eventual success since it would draw him oftener to Leeson-street and he would naturally be anxious for the company of his friend in such a delicate situation. Then he would have a better chance of studying Morna and her life without making his object too glaringly apparent.

"Is flirtation your aim or do you aspire to anything more serious, Arthur?"

"Gad, a fellow can't be expected to know so much at a moment's notice. I'm not certain that I'd be making such a big fool of myself if I did go in for her seriously. I'd be giving up Evy's money, but this little thing is more a lady in face and manner, and she's a damned sight more unusual too. Didn't Fairfax the other day marry an Irish girl without family or money, and, by Jove, Denny, all the fellows fell dead in love with her and thought him the luckiest fellow out, though she hadn't a sixpence and wasn't half as pretty as Marjory."

"Well, Arthur, if you are serious, I can only say I wish you every success, and I cordially admire your choice," said Denzil gravely. "I'm at your disposal if you want to begin proceedings to-day."

When they arrived at Leeson-street they found Marjory deliberating if she would go down to her office or not. Their appearance solved the problem, and she remained in to receive them.

"If you want to see Morna you must come at about seven," she explained. "She is never home before dinner-hour."

Marjory's presence of course charmed Brecknock. Denzil was very considerate. He pored over Marjory's scrap-album, made himself dull from a conversational point of view; studied photographs and views with exemplary assiduity, and left Arthur nothing to complain of on the ground of interference. Marjory was in brilliant spirits; Frank was to spend that evening with her, and he had not alluded to his governor or to his allowance since. She dashed into talk with her usual exuberance and unseizable wit, until Brecknock gazed on her in fair bewilderment. He alluded to the arrest of Hamilton, and she told him she was going to see him at Kilmainham.

"'Pon my word, Miss Maurice, I'd given a good deal to go with you. I wonder now would you consent to take me."

"Take you, Mr. Brecknock! An officer in her Majesty's service! Of course I will. It would be really a delightful joke."

"Oh, I don't mean it as a joke; but seriously, I rather liked that friend of yours," Brecknock hastened to explain, with his grave side-glance. "What day shall it be, Miss Maurice?"

"Well, you must come and see Morna first. It will depend on her chiefly."

"Oh, I've heard from Evy Handcock that you can twist her round your finger, as it seems to me you can twist anybody. Just you persuade her to make a party of it, and let Denny and myself be your escorts. Den would like it, and,'pon my soul, I'd like nothing better," he urged, in his calm insistence."

"Let me add my entreaties to my friend's. I would be really interested in seeing Kilmainham and an Irish political prisoner," joined in Dalrymple, archly.

"This is really wonderful," laughed Marjory. "Why, I'll believe next we shall send you back to the Adversary even Land Leaguers, perhaps organisers. If you come some day after I've seen Morna, I shall be able to make an appointment for going to Kilmainham."

The young man seized on the opportunity and called the next day. Morna was, of course, at the office, and Marjory, after some entreaty, consented to take them down to Sackville-street in search of her.

"But you mustn't look like strangers," she added outside, while Brecknock was gazing admiringly at her coquettish little hat. "When you enter the office you must have the appearance of having been there before. In fact, try to look like Prisoners' Aid young men."[49]

"Who are they? asked Dalrymple.

"Young men who give us money for the prisoners, of course," explained Marjory.

CHAPTER XIII

THE VISIT TO THE OFFICE.

It was an hour when the office was fullest. Marjory led the way upstairs into the outer-room, where a half-dozen of girls were busy writing and examining papers and documents at side and centre tables, and one solitary male individual was folding large parcels. Those facing the door looked up at Marjory, and nodding, curiously examined the young men following her.

"There is the male official of the Ladies' Land League," whispered Marjory to her companions, as they bent to catch her words in eager curiosity, like boys on their first tour drinking in the guide's observations. "I call him the first gentleman in Europe. You've no idea how distinguished and finished he is; when he wants stamps he bows as gravely as the chief himself, and says—'Madam, I beg to state that the stamps are exhausted.'"

The young men looked at the official, and then round the room with a weakly-interested smile, astonished to find themselves in such a place, and very much afraid of not conducting themselves with becoming decorum.

"I once went to see my sister at a girl's school, and she insisted on my doing the classes, and I felt bad, I can tell you, but, by Jove, feel a thousand times worse now," said Brecknock, in an undertone.

---

49. 'A special group was formed within the Ladies' Land League to help prisoners and their families; this was called the "Political Prisoners' Aid Society"' (O'Neill 1982, p. 129).

"Come inside now; this is the inner chamber, and of course private. Walk straight over to Morna as if you had business with her; but whatever you do don't have the air of spies or sight-seers," said Marjory opening the door, while her companions felt as uncomfortably expectant as if they were about to be ushered into a meeting of savages. Denzil's pulses shook a little nervously, it would be so laughable, he thought, if it were not quite so strange. "Look at her attentively, and perhaps she will look up. I'll tell you who she is afterwards."

Denzil glanced in the direction and looked away as quickly in search of Morna. There were about twelve ladies—mostly girls—with heads bent earnestly over account-books, letters, prison and eviction forms, and all working with incredible energy to those not accustomed to associate women with a capacity for serious official work. Arthur, with his drawl and indolent carriage, was observant enough to see that the room held many pretty faces and attractive figures, which contrasted oddly, to his thinking, with ledgers, books, and blue envelopes.

"By Jove, how serious they all are," he thought; "and what the devil can so many find to write about? I never thought there was a woman under the sun who could find any interest or amusement in being cooped up in an office plaguing away at that kind of thing."

"Do you mean to say they go on like this every day?" he asked of Marjory.

"Every day and evening as well. You have no idea how much there is to be done, and what hard work it is. That's our treasurer. Isn't she pretty? There's the young lady who has the care of the prisoners. See how pale and delicate-looking men in the aggregate can make one little woman when food is in question. There, the lady I showed you has raised her eyes. Take a good look at her, do."

At that moment Denzil had finished his vain search for Morna's striking face, and was listening. He looked, too, and saw a delicate, white face, with grey eyes, steadily examining him.[50]

"Come. We shall find Morna in Gardiner-street Church.[51] This is Saturday, her day for Confession," said Marjory, walking towards the door, with a pleasant greeting for everyone.

"I want Morna to come to Kilmainham with me to see Hamilton," she stopped to say to one of her friends, a marvel of energy and spirits, who never did less than two things at once, and both remarkably well.

"I don't think she will. She's in one of her heavy-tenth-century moods," was the answer. "However, if you are going up to Kilmainham you may as well take up those flowers sent today for Parnell, Dillon, and O'Kelly.[52] Of course, they'll fume and rage when they get the flowers; all men do; but that's nothing to you, and they must put up with the inconveniences of political martyrdom or notoriety."

Marjory lifted up the bouquets and gravely handed one to each officer.

"By Jove," cried Brecknock, eying the thing thrust into his hand in strong disapproval.

"You don't mean to say you expect us to carry these things through the streets, Miss Maurice?"

"How stupid of me. I was forgetting we had to go to Gardiner-street first," she laughed, giving the flowers into the care of the grave official in the outer room till their return.

---

50. A first glimpse of Georgiana – modelled on Anna Parnell.
51. St Francis Xavier's church, popularly known as Gardiner Street Church. Noted for its architectural elegance and collection of artworks, it features in James Joyce's later short story *Grace*. https://www.buildingsofireland.ie/buildings-search/building/50010824/saint-francis-xavier-church-gardiner-street-upper-dublin-dublin
52. Charles Stewart Parnell (1846–91, politician); John Dillon MP (1851–1927), nationalist parliamentarian; James Joseph O'Kelly (1842–1916), Fenian, journalist, and politician). See the *Dictionary of Irish Biography* for full biographical details and Niamh O'Sullivan's *Every Dark Hour: A History of Kilmainham Jail* (2007) for the full list of those imprisoned and conditions in the prison.

They knocked at the Presbytery and learnt that Morna was still in the church.

While they were deliberating about sending for her, or going in search of her themselves, Frank Harston and a Jesuit appeared in the hall. Marjory's face lit up, and she cried, impulsively:

"Frank!"

"How do you do, Miss Maurice?" said Harston, in the bland medium of mere acquaintance and friendship, and, after casual observations on her health, the political situation, and the weather, which rather bewildered her, and a cold recognition of her companions, passed on.

"Is that young lady a friend of yours, Frank?" asked Father Trediger, with an inquiring look.

"Hardly a friend. I know her uncle a little, and have met her a few times," he answered carelessly.

"If I don't mistake I think she called you Frank," returned the priest.

"Damn it!" muttered Harston. "Oh, she is one of those girls who make a practice of calling every fellow they meet a second time by their Christian names. A nice little girl, but an abominable little flirt. I believe she is engaged to one of those fellows."

It was the first time Denzil had been inside a Catholic church since he had returned from abroad. "The contemplation of such sweet motherhood as that," he mused, "not as a picture, but as a part of daily belief and aspiration, the sweeter for its familiar presence, cannot be without its beneficial effect on women." And then he remembered the grave, clear purity of Morna's eyes; the firm, strong face, paled into spirituality; and the Madonna-like pensiveness and sweetness of her smile. And there was that living ideal of the old Catholic Madonna approaching him, grey-robed, but wearing now no smile, and with prayer still on her mute lips. His pulses beat quickly and gladly as he turned to the door. He looked at the pictures of St. Ignatius and St. Francis Borgia, and beyond of St. Francis Xavier dying a soldier's death for his cause, and concluded that there was a great deal to be proud of in the Catholic Faith.[53] Surely, it was symbolical of courage and grand endurance, and if Morna would give up politics, he at least could promise to respect and admire her religion. But, would she ever come to care for his love? he wondered, looking at her as she held out her hand to him with a surprised look. She seemed like an ideal of womanhood—half-maiden, half-mother, apart from any one man's possession, rather than a girl to be wooed and won as girls are.

"Your sister, Miss Maurice, actually led us into treasonable practices to-day," he said, as Marjory and Brecknock walked on in advance, Marjory looking even graceful brushing the steps down with her swift, light feet. "Fancy two lieutenants of her Majesty's navy in the very heart of the feminine enemy! in no place less terrible than the office of the Ladies' Land League, and now on our way to Kilmainham to visit a suspect."

Before Morna could answer Marjory tripped back and asked Denzil:

"Did you notice the lady I pointed out to you? What did you think of her?"

"That she, like all of you, very little resembles the orthodox conception of a strong-minded woman? Her eyes are strikingly clear and honest—and steady. I don't think she would trouble herself much about small offences, but she would be very stern in judging wrong-doing or injustice."

"What do you think of her as our own chieftainess?"[54]

"What! that pale, delicately-featured, and frail girl! She surely hasn't a frame to meet eviction scenes and outdoor meetings! I'm amazed. Pretty and fragile-looking, with a proud, cold little face so unlike that of an agitator's."

---

53. These paintings are included in Father Matthew Russell's article: 'The New Pictures in St. Francis Xavier's, Dublin'. *The Irish Monthly*, 9, no. 101 (1881): pp. 606–13. www.jstor.org/stable/20496659.
54. Charles Parnell was referred to as the 'Chief'.

(To be Continued – Commenced in No. 949.)

Vol. XXII. – No. 956.
Saturday, February 7, 1885: pp. 292–294.

CHAPTER XIV

KILMAINHAM – THE RESERVED SQUADRON.

Outside the prison they had ample time to walk up and down in the fresh, spring sunshine, as the prisoners were at dinner. Then the rusty key was turned by an old warder known to many as the Grizzled Bear, for the very obvious reason that his beard and hair were grizzled, and his manner refreshingly bearish. Marjory had discovered the way to the heart of this morose janitor, which lay in a frequent use of the prefix Mr. when addressing him.

"Can we see Mr. Hamilton, Mr. Martin?" she asked, in her blandest manner.

"Mr. Hamilton. You want to see Mr. Hamilton? All right. Take a seat."

"And these bouquets are for Mr. Parnell, Mr. Dillon, and Mr. O'Kelly. Their names and those of the donors are attached, Mr. Martin."[55]

She pointed out each and its respective destiny. He took the bouquets.

"I see. Mr. Parnell, Mr. Dillon, and Mr. O'Kelly," he said, pointing to each with his finger, and unconsciously altering the names. "That's all right. Mr. O'Kelly, Mr. Parnell, and Mr. Dillon. Who did you ask to see?"

---

55. In his memoir, *Kilmainham Memories*, Tighe Hopkins records the treatment of Parnell and other Land League members, noting how the 'Ladies' Land League kept their table furnished with the best' (1896, p. 16), listing the gifts sent by admirers, including flowers (p. 26).

"Mr. Hamilton," said Marjory.

"Mr. Hamilton; yes, that's all right. Mr. Dillon, Mr. Parnell, Mr. O'Kelly. Didn't you say you wanted to see somebody? he asked, coming back.

"Didn't the young lady say Mr. Hamilton twice already?" interrupted a younger warder, with a shrug.

"Did you say Mr. Hamilton?" persisted the old man. "Oh, yes, I remember now; he hasn't been visited to-day. Let me see; these are for—who did you say?"

Marjory instructed him again in perfect gravity, and he shook his head. Eventually the flowers were incorrectly delivered, but, as they came from perfectly impartial admirers, it probably was no matter of importance. At that moment a warder appeared to conduct them to Mr. Hamilton.

"You read the notice, ladies and gentlemen, and, of course, you'll not put me to the extremely unpleasant task of interrupting your conversation," said the courteous representation of British rule.

Brecknock raised an ornamental eye-glass and inspected the notice to keep clear of politics or treasonable subjects.

"By jove this is a good joke for us, Den. Supposing they arrested us as suspects! Wouldn't it be jolly?"

"I believe you have turned an army man into a raging Land Leaguer?" said Denzil to Morna.

"Yes; it only remains now for you to give the navy good example," smiled Morna.

The warder stared at the men in surprise.

"There is Mr. Hamilton," he said, moving aside to let them stand in front of the outer bars of the human cage few Irish people are not now familiar with.

The young men were too busy staring down into the hall where the suspects were exercising and round at similar constructions in which these political hosts received their guests top remark at first the gentleman waiting to receive them.

He wore a dark red smoking cap, which he lifted as the girls came in sight, his worn and pallid face made a double radiance in dark glance and deep, swift flush as he held Morna's hand and gave his eyes a mute embrace of that familiar face.

"You were long about coming, Morna, but I know you have much to think of, and that you could not forget me. Each day I hoped would bring you to me to tell me that you are satisfied with me this once."

"When did I give you to understand that I was dissatisfied in anything you have done? You know I think well of you in all things but one."

"And that?" he asked hurriedly in a lower tone as he saw Denzil turn round from his inspection.

"In your folly in thinking that anything can be better and wiser than real friendship. Mr. Dalrymple, allow me to introduce you to my friend, Mr. Hamilton." Denzil shook hands with him very cordially, Brecknock following with a limper salutation, but Hamilton was coldly reserved and distrustful. Why should these fellows have the privilege of escorting Morna to see him locked up and powerless in prison, and one of them in such striking contrast with him, younger, probably richer, handsome and brilliant-looking? Of course he did not really fear such shallow attractions would be likely to gather the wonderful and untouched treasure of Morna's love. But women, the best of them, have been known to do such strange things, to fall in love so mysteriously. How could she ever answer for herself if the "man-milliner" should prove her destiny? Absurd!

"Did you hear that Harley has got into an awful row with the Orangemen? He made a furious speech in Belmullet yesterday," cried Marjory.[56]

---

56. Orangemen: generically associated with Unionists or Protestants of Ulster. In this particular context the allusion is most likely connected with the 'boycotting' of Captain Boycott in Co. Mayo and the recruiting of labourers by Orange politicians to help harvest the estate produce in November 1881. Co. Mayo was 'the birthplace of the Land League and league agitation in the country' (Lucey 2011, p. 585). The news of an 'Affray at Belmullet', a small town in Mayo, featured in various papers at this time.

"Pray, miss, remember the notice," said the warder with an apologetic smile.

"Will it be reasonable to mention that her Majesty is in the enjoyment of excellent health, and that she drove out to-day accompanied by the Princess Beatrice, and Marchioness of Ely?" she asked gravely. After that the conversation was strictly personal, not to mention a few sarcasms thrown out for the benefit of the warder, and with a promise to return soon they left Hamilton to his dreary reflections. It was two o'clock when the officers drove from Sackville-street, where they left Marjory and Morna. Frank's curious manner that morning left the former too dull and vaguely depressed for anything like work. She remembered it was some weeks since she had seen Evelyn Handcock and resolved on paying her a visit and inducing her to come to see the Reserved Squadron on view outside the harbour. Evelyn was in a brilliantly rakish mood, and the mad proposal fascinated her. At first she thought of asking Brecknock to escort them, but neither he nor his friend had been there lately, and it would be clearly undignified to pursue such hopelessly indifferent suitors.

"What harm? It'll be all the jollier alone. We can flirt the more," she said, as they made their way down to the jetty where the "Safety" was on its last run to the Fleet. They purchased their tickets, and felt far from comfortable in the rickety vessel, sarcastically named.

"My papa would be out of his mind if he knew this, and 'pon my word I don't think Morna would like it a bit better," cried Evelyn, in her high soprano.

Of course, there was nobody on the "Safety" worth flirting with—so her glances and delightful exclamations were kept in reserve for the officers of the "Centaur". As she ran down the companion steps in advance of Marjory, she cried to a sailor:

"Whether are we fore or aft?"

"Fore, ma'am," answered the sailor.

"Come aft, then, Marjory," she called, making at once for the officer's quarters.

Marjory followed, unconsciously staring round the vessel with curious eyes.

"Can we pass," asked Evelyn in a loud voice, and smiling audaciously, as she raised a red cord railing off the officer's quarters.

"Most certainly," said a bland young middy, ushering them down to the smoking-room.

Evelyn walked on boldly, stood in the centre of the apartment, and gave one of her effective silvery laughs, when she saw a crowd of men smoking and drinking whisky or brandy-and-water, in long tumblers. The sight startled Marjory, and she ran back, but Evelyn called to her, holding the curtain in her hand while she addressed one of the officers, who had advanced familiarly to offer her a cigarette.

"It is all right, isn't it?" she laughed.

"You flatter us deeply, madam. You won't have a cigarette? Then I won't press you. Perhaps you will favour us with a waltz? he said, approaching and opening a piano, winking at his companions as he did so.

"My friend plays better than I do. Marjory, won't you play?" said Evelyn.

"Oh, no," said Marjory, in cold reproach.

"You hold your favours dearly," sneered the officer, and Marjory walked away with a face of scarlet.

"See how complaisant I am. I'll let you escort me over your vessel," said Evelyn.

With another expressive wink at his companions he walked out with her, and mockingly assumed the air of a cicerone.

"You see that? that's a lamp; and this is a baby-gun. A baby-gun, a lamp; and this here is a water-jar. It holds water usually, but now it is empty."

"You'll tell me next, I hope, that you're a man and I'm a woman," she laughed, with an audacious swoop of her eyes.

"Ah! that topic would be something more to the purpose. You

see this gangway? I unfortunately cannot go any further with you as I'm on duty, which ends here and it is a breach of rule to go beyond it. You can do so if you like. Most happy to have had the pleasure," he added, bowing and hiding himself behind a huge cannon till she had disappeared and given him a chance of getting back unobserved by her to the smoke-room. As he had guessed, she addressed herself to another officer who, after a few blank civilities, found suddenly that duty forbade him to move another step in the service of beauty. Marjory caught a glimpse of both afterwards looking down from the poop and convulsed in hearty laughter. In her wild anxiety to get off the vessel, she left her friend's side to see if the "Safety" was yet in sight, and when she came back she found a young middy explaining to Evelyn that an officer named Etherton believed he was acquainted with her, and would be glad to see her downstairs. Marjory remonstrated, but Evelyn insisted on seeing Etherton, though the name was perfectly strange to her, and down she went. Of course, it was the practical joke of a half dozen midshipmen who dragged up a giggling young paymaster's clerk to confront him with this dashing Roiville flirt. The youth behaved like a schoolboy, and even Evelyn at last flushed angrily. She was mollified, however, when the chief mover in the joke offered his service in atonement, and conducted her to the least frequented part of the vessel, Marjory following with eyes wet with tears of shame. Here he flirted a bit, looked wonderingly at the pale, cold, silent little girl, and then conducted them on deck to await the "Safety," with personal observations neither witty nor original enough to merit repetition, and added to the list of those who had bid them farewell on the plea of "duty," to laugh at them from a vantage point. Marjory was wistfully thinking of Frank, and what folly his unkindness had led her into. But she vowed she would never again see Evelyn Handcock nor a man-of-war.

"Such a stupid day! Those fellows are awfully idiotic, really. Herbert Hamilton is worth a dozen of them. That reminds me, he's in Kilmainham. I must go to see him, dear fellow," exclaimed

Evelyn, arranging her bracelets carefully.

"He will be delighted to see you, I'm sure," said Marjory, in what she felt dreary sarcasm.

"Well, Marge, have you been moving any important resolutions to-day?" asked her uncle, seating himself in his arm-chair in that large way of his which implied that he was committing an action at once condescending and amazingly comfortable for himself; of course he had the habits of such men at home—of rubbing his hands a little before thrusting them into capacious and unmentionable pockets, and looking around with the lazy, self-satisfied smile of the man who has made his own fortune (so peculiarly irritating to the poor devil who has a fortune to make, and sees very dim possibilities, and still slighter chances, of accomplishing that desirable end); of standing on the hearth-rug with his coat-tails parted, his back to the fire, and his legs rather wider apart than would be quite admissible in our ideal of the Apollo Belvidere.[57] Who doesn't know the attitude?

"It has been a day of adventures, uncle."

"To begin with, little woman."

"I brought two officers down to the office, then to Gardiner-street Church, in search of Morna, who was at confession; then to Kilmainham, to see Hamilton."

"The Lord deliver us! You brought those young fellows about like that. They're rather well in their way. I always thought that kind of animal was more or less of a cad, but I declare I admire the chap you call Dalrymple. The other one drawls so infernally, and insists on sticking up that impudent-looking eye-glass when I know he wants it about just as much as I do; besides, he's a bit of an idiot. But he is of a very good family, and I'm curious enough to know why he's taken up with us," he said meditatively.

"Oh, uncle, how unpenetrating! Don't you see he's desperately in love with me?"

---

57. Celebrated marble sculpture of the Greek god Apollo in a distinctive pose.

"You little witch! 'Pon my word, I wouldn't be surprised you'll be giving up Harston for him one of these days. That reminds me, is he coming here this evening?"

"Who? Frank?" she asked, with a little start and a swift flush of delicate pink. "I think not; no."

He did not see the look of pain that started into the cool, blue eyes under the long, drooped lashes which caught a deeper tinge from the firelight. She felt her mouth was trembling foolishly, and she bent her head lower under her clasped hands to hide it from her uncle.

"I'm blessed if I understand the lovemaking of to-day. In my time there was less shilly-shallying and dangling, and, upon my word, I think the young men and women were much the better and more comfortable for it. I never wanted you to rush off and engage yourself to that fellow at all, but, faith, when you did, I can't for the life of me see why you couldn't have made shorter work of it; and I'd like to know why Harston comes so irregularly. Have you been quarrelling with him?"

"No – that is, yes; a little. Didn't you ever have a lover's quarrel, uncle?" she asked, piteously, catching her breath in a short, silent sob.

"Yes, but it seems to be nothing but lovers' quarrels with you since he came up from Wicklow. Once in a way, I dare say it's highly interesting, especially the making up that. Bless you! I haven't forgotten the way I felt the first time I kissed the girl I had quarrelled with."

"That's just the way with us," she laughed; but the notes trembled and quivered with the weight of unshed tears. "We take such a perilous delight in reconciliation that we quarrel every time we meet for the mere pleasure of making up again. But you didn't ask me the rest of my adventures. Evy Handcock and I were on board the 'Centaur' today."

"Those fellows brought you over, of course."

"No, they didn't."

"What, did old Handcock act the escort to a pair of flirts like you and Evy?"

"No."

"Then who the devil brought you?"

"No one; we went ourselves."

"Do you wish me to believe, Marjory, that you actually visited the 'Centaur' with nobody but that rowdy madcap?" asked Mr. Maurice, sternly and slowly.

"Yes," was the answer from the drooped, sad little head.

"Listen to me, Marjory. I never approved of your acquaintance with that fast school companion of yours. I never saw what she could want with you, or you with her; you were both in different spheres and had a right to keep in them. I wish you now to understand that it is my express with that this objectionable acquaintance should cease. Do you hear me? and can I trust you to obey me?"

"I was ashamed and angry myself afterwards, and meant not to visit her again," said Marjory, still with bent head and averted face.

CHAPTER XV

MARJORY'S LOVE-TROUBLE.

Spring rushed with light, passionate swiftness into summer's embrace. A more beautiful Eastertide than that of '81 could not well be imagined. And May had gone tremblingly into June, and then at last July turned chilly and irresponsive after the first fond ardour of the meeting. Though the land was heated by political passion, the cool airs of heaven swept over it; the sunrise and sunset flushes from east to west bathed it in tremulous and varying radiances, and the rain-clouds of misty blue, of those indescribable tints where violet and crimson meet, of rose as tender as childhood's cheek and of diaphanous white, cast their shadows on the hillsides and plains which respond to their moods with a sympathy that depends the significance of their beauty.

The prisons all over the country were clearing fast. The people were beginning to shake themselves out of the passionate, half-hysterical fright into which the famous Park murders had thrown them, and were probably decorously conscious of having, in and out of Parliament, through newspapers which wept admirably in the deepest possible mourning, through public votes of condolence and members of the Imperial Parliament, who spoke their emotion and distress in muffled tones—or at least were represented as doing such to a satisfied nation, naturally insistent on retrieving its honour—expressed in the fittest way their horror of what was really one of Ireland's cruellest blows.[58] We know the Conservative Press rushed frantically at the Land Leaguers—some going the length even of accusing the Ladies' Land League of having participated in the outrage. Delicate and fragile women, with clear consciences and sweet natures—some of them young and light-hearted girls—were represented by the most rabid of their enemies as actual murderers, while others were content with the milder accusation of conspiracy.[59] It is laughable now; it was laughable then to those who were acquainted with the members of that most energetic, earnest-working, and enthusiastic organisation. I write of the Ladies' Land League as a mere spectator, as one who, a member, was entirely dissociated from

---

58. Phoenix Park Murders: 'Late in the afternoon of 6 May 1882 Lord Frederick Cavendish, newly appointed chief secretary for Ireland, and Thomas Burke, his under-secretary, were walking in Phoenix Park (Dublin) when four men leapt from a cab and stabbed them to death. Soon afterwards newspaper offices in Dublin received black-edged cards, claiming the outrage for a nationalist group called the "Irish Invincibles"'. Cannon, John, and Robert Crowcroft. Phoenix Park murders'. *A Dictionary of British History.* Oxford University Press. Oxford Reference. <https://www.oxfordreference.com/view/10.1093/acref/9780191758027.001.0001/acref-9780191758027-e-2720>.
59. Members of the Ladies' Land League were accused of having links to the murders in the British press, and Hannah Lynch was named as one of the murder ring in an article on the 'Fenian Conspiracy' published in *John Bull* magazine (10 July 1886, p. 446). For further details see Binckes and Laing 2019, pp. 51–52.

such genuine and hard work as the most insignificant member of it accomplished in Sackville-street. A recent effort in literature has branded them with a cruel injustice—as frivolous, notoriety-hunting, and unwomanly.[60] The formation of that body—though a deeply regrettable fact for its own sake–served, if nothing else, to prove to those who were just enough to recognise it—not many of those!—that a woman may work as hard as any man, with a conscientiousness every true woman brings into work once chosen, however distasteful it may be, disinterestedly, since they, unlike their fellow-workers, can never hope to achieve fame by labours of that nature, and keep within her, warm, the sweetest fibres of womanliness and tenderness. I do not think I personally knew a lady Land Leaguer who was not kinder to her sex, more upright, and more earnest—a little excitable, if you will, in some cases, where youth and high, fresh spirits justified excitement—more generous and true-hearted, than most I have met with under more usual circumstances. I like to record the pleasant fact as a tribute to much natural goodness, that has been so falsely coloured.

At the time I write of Dublin was thrilled into a different kind of excitement, political, still, but speculative and commercial.

I refer to the Exhibition.[61] It was the first week of August, and already the streets were filling rapidly, and assuming a bright and expectant look – not precisely that of acquired prosperity, but that of prosperity reaching forward through dissolving gloom in hopeful shapeliness. It was an event of immense moment. Bets ran high on its failure and success, since it was to be purely a national speculation.

I mention these two facts in recent history: the Park Tragedy and the Exhibition, because they both bear on the personal history

---

60. A likely reference to Fanny Gallaher's *Thy Name is Truth*. See Binckes and Laing 2019, pp. 52–53.
61. 'On 15th August 1882 [the] Dublin exhibition of art and industries was opened in the Rotunda Hospital gardens and visited by 261,205 people' (Turpin 1982, p. 48).

of my little blonde heroine we left last March with drooping eyelashes, hiding the pain beneath, with fluttering and aching heart-throbs, and repressed, apprehensive sobs staying her utterance. It promised to be soon a desolate figure then, and the promise would have been fulfilled but for the intense interest of the times.

Harston had not been as expeditive as he proposed in coming back to Dublin. Out of the distracting influence of Marjory's presence or nearness, he could plan his course of action in admirable cold-bloodedness. But knowing that whenever he went out he ran the risk of confronting her poor, pathetic, small face, the more touching from its resolutely repressed pain and proud smile, naturally lowered the temperature of his courage. Miss Trediger's style was massive; he certainly could not hold her in his arms as he could Marjory's fairy-like form, nor were her lips—pale with the suggestion of heaviness—formed for Juliet-like ardour of confession like Marjory's: red as cherries, small as a bird's, drooping into the little white cheeks with a hint of pathos in their abruptness. Then Miss Trediger's eyes were painfully uninteresting, and, by Jove! the mere thought of Marjory's—were there ever eyes so big and blue and star-like?—made his breath come hurriedly. These were things a young man must think of twice before relinquishing even in his own interest. And Harston thought of them a little oftener than twice. At last in Easter Week he could stand it no longer, and fled on pretence of having to eat his dinners in London. The excuse sounded natural, and no suspicions were awakened in the commercial breast of Mr. Maurice. Marjory was filled with presentiments, but then girls always are filled with vague presentiments when Fate (?) parts them from their lovers. Happily the world pays as little heed to their nonsensical fancies as their lovers do.

At first Morna laughed her fears away. Was it death she was thinking of? Surely she could not love him if she doubted his truth! So Marjory hid her silent dread, and laughed and chatted with her friends as of old. Frank corresponded irregularly, but as that is the admitted privilege of men after a certain stage in amatory existence, she did her best to still the heart-pang throbbing within her, and imitated his irregularity and brevity. I cannot assert that she found a necessity for brevity a particular hardship, for she was not fond of writing, and held long letters, whether to be read or written, in especial detestation. But his letters were ambiguous, and a girl of her direct and simple nature was distressed and terrified before ambiguity. Then came a time—in May, when the lanes were blossoming into hawthorn and the song of birds so thick through the hedges that they nearer approached touch than sound—when no letters arrived. A paper first, which gradually ceased; a long silence—for poor Marjory a long lent of the heart, fed on excitement and breathless wonder from outside. Historical events hurried her along so long [sic] quickly that she had scarcely time to understand her own great sorrow. Then, too, there was Hamilton to be visited and soothed, since he, too, had his burden of hopeless pain to carry. There were Brecknock and Dalrymple to entertain and amuse; Brecknock too saliently in love, but still not to be repulsed, since declaration was not forthcoming, and—why criticise? She found his homage a soothing reparation for another's slight. She was not so much a coquette as a delicate, irresponsible fabric of gossamer whims. Then, too, there was Denzil Dalrymple to analyse, wonder at, speculate on; his frequent visits, the silent largeness of his gaze when Morna was within its focus; his dreamy, meditative ways dashed with a kind of briny metaphysics, so whirlingly following a mystifying explosive jollity. All these things were to be thought out and classified, for Marjory's was a curious mixture of large-mindedness and egoism. She sorrowed horribly over her own ills; but that did not, nevertheless, blind her to what was going on around her, and made her no less keen and anxious to trace effects to their remotest causes. She was sharp, we know, and few escaped her sharpness, which we will not call unerring. Then there was the satisfaction of cutting Evelyn Handcock, who had so wounded her pride and girl's respect on that memorable visit to the "Centaur"; there was the generous *camaraderie* in Sackville-street, and Power's delicately-inferred adoration breathing through his wild anecdotes and stories. On the whole, the summer was pleasant withal, when a message from Frank startled her.

(To be Continued – Commenced in No. 949.)

Vol. XXII. – No. 957.
Saturday, February 14, 1885: 308–310.

CHAPTER XVI

A MESSAGE FROM FRANK – HAMILTON'S MOOD.

By the evening post came a short letter from Harston, stating that he expected to be over in Dublin for the opening of the Exhibition, but that he could not promise to remain long, as his governor expected him down in Wicklow, where he had made arrangements to stay over. The letter was not much, would have been bitter even for that reference to Wicklow, where there was some horrible matrimonial speculation, but there came with it a very dangerous special pleader—a cabinet likeness of this Proteus. It was a splendid likeness; you might fancy yourself listening for the voice; for the sound of the breathing, waiting to see the eyelids move. Even on the dull pasteboard the eyes seemed to sparkle with life, and the mouth looked eager to break into its familiar smile. Poor little Marjory's stoicism was shattered. Was coldness possible with that image of love in her hand or pressed to her lips? She would not acknowledge it, certainly not; imagine the backward toss of the head, and the resolute compression of the little mouth here, that sudden rigidity of the elastic figure which so emphatically expresses "no"; but could she be expected to make any promise to herself that she would not forgive him when he came. Her sleep was a mere pretence that night. It was scarcely six o'clock when she rose, satisfied that joy had done services for sleep. She went out into the narrow slip of garden bounded by the unused stables. The sky was one vast indistinctness of grey and russet brown; a cold, sad sky, where even eastwards showed no red or promise of colour, and through this immeasurable veil the pale starpoints glimmered faintly, rather as linking night to dawn before they quite passed away into memory. The silence of the city at that hour is mysteriously deep. The merest sound sets one wondering, so vivid in the rush through the fresh, delicate air; at no other time does one get more thoroughly at the very heart of silence and solitude; even the winds are unfamiliar, so untainted, so piercing, as though they came from far above the mountains, and had not time to gather warmth from plain and valley. The grasses and leaves of the garden were wet and grey in the thick dew-mists, and the mad, panting songs of the birds were swept citywards on the clear air till you might almost fancy a whole hedge-full close beside you.

These things did not touch Marjory minutely, but even their vague effect cannot be otherwise than beneficial. She wet her shoes in the moist grasses, and shuddered pleasantly, for she was too happy to care about the cold. There were a great many scenes in connection with this garden. She remembered distinctly the day she and Frank walked along that outer path, and after a slight difference born of mutual irritating jealousy, Frank stopped and caressed her beside that laurel bush. She was fond of laurels even afterwards. And then the evening they were going to the theatre and she brought him out here to gather some purple pansies, which she insisted he should wear to match those nestling against her throat. Yes, memories floated thickly through the air in this garden; memories of gestures, looks, attitudes, light or fond caresses, and words of endearment. Nonsense, if you will; but these are the gamut of joy in courtship, and there are few churlish enough to deny that such trivialities are laden with subtle language, catching personality from the associations they stir. To the happy of the moment they flow like rich and tender music, but to most they bring a smile not so much of pity as of remembered illusions.

How much she would have to tell Frank. Would she make him jealous by referring to Brecknock? Ah, no; she was tired of teasing him. To be sure, it would not be amiss to let him see that his conduct and absence had not turned her into an Ariadne-like figure of desolation. She was never of that type, thank God, and men are somewhat prone to exult in the belief that one or two women's hearts are throbbing in pain and forlornness for them. Certainly, Marjory was justified in taking some pride to herself that she had not dwelt apart in sorrowful maidenhood. She had flirted pretty freely with Brecknock; went twice with her uncle to the "Adversary" At Homes; was greatly pleased in the knowledge that she looked charming, and that everyone admired her; practised with Brecknock's air-pistol in the garden with the stable for their target, while Denzil and Morna looked on and sometimes took part in the shooting; laughed and blushed and flung out her bubbling wit and mimickery [sic] with a spontaneity much resembling a bird's singing or a stream's gurgling. You no more thought of asking how the one was done than the others. And if her eyes were just a little bigger and wistfuller, no one saw it but Morna, who watched in silence. This courage deserved boasting of, and she half made up her mind to make Frank feel bad by telling him of it. Marjory had picked up a few Americanisms which she enjoyed; delighted in speaking of when she or anybody "felt bad," or had "chills and fever all the time." But at present she recognised that she was running a fair chance of giving herself chills and fever of some sort, and as she heard Kate stirring inside, she thought that the flow of a kitchen fire would be a pleasant variety.

Hamilton had been released early in June. His life since then had not altered visibly in its main headings. He was not quite so strong, and began to develop laziness; he wrote less, and spent more time in Leeson-street than he had ever done before. Some time ago Marjory would have been irritated at Morna's persistent irresponsiveness to his suit, but now she hailed it with pleasure—carefully veiled from Hamilton's jealous glance—since it led her to build hopes on a more brilliant match for her sister. She was very fond of Herbert Mercer after a fashion; regarded him as a huge, learned, practical joke, and thought herself a marvel of goodness and consideration because she was content to sit beside him and soothe him with her brightest stories while his eyes looked dreamily out of their lazy observation. He was pleased with Marjory's attentions: they stilled his passionate need of those others he hungered after. He hated Denzil with a lover's unreasoning hate. Why should Morna take such interest in that fellow's nonsensical chatter? He heard him talk to her one evening about "John Inglesant". In the name of goodness, where had he picked up with "John Inglesant", and how was it that he was actually brilliant and earnest in discussing it? And he was even not ashamed to profess a tender reverence for "Daniel Deronda," and brought a deepening lustre into Morna's beautiful, serene eyes over the mournful struggles of poor Gwendolen.[62] Hamilton was furious, and went home and bemused himself over a borrowed copy of "Daniel Deronda," which he confessed to himself he could make nothing of; thought Deronda an ineffable prig; Gwendolen an anomaly; and wondered greatly how she could have encouraged that fellow to spout his nonsense, and act the part of a ruffian towards herself; found Grandcourt an exaggeration of bloodlessness, and Mordecai had the effect of a nightmare on him. Clearly the book would not bring out any counter eloquence from him, and that severe sarcasm of his, the value of which none knew better than he, would only serve to distress Morna after the infernally sentimental impressions that fellow's rubbish had left on her mind. "Oh, these women," he reflected bitterly. "It only needs a little mock-sentiment, a neat reference to the inner consciousness, a touch of trouble or conflict, the shallowest assumption of generous

---

62. Gwendolen Harleth: central female protagonist in George Eliot's *Daniel Deronda* (1876).

aspiration, to turn the most commonplace fellow into a hero, a martyr, a saint in their illusive gaze! Look at a girl like Morna even answering a mere idiot's incomprehensible allusions to wavering faith—stuff and nonsense! a good thrashing would have cured him—the supreme effect of one good nature emitting goodness and blessing and beauty by mere fact of its own being; quoting a mad American poet about following whoever speaks to him in the right voice as the moon follows the stream silently. Whoever heard of such a simile? And Morna could listen to that rubbish and not sicken at it! Ouf! such platitudes, such transcendental humbug! And not only listen, but respond to his insolently direct gaze with those large simple eyes of hers shining with the faith and wonder of purest, tenderest womanhood! If he only had the chance of knocking the fellow down, with his insipid gold hair and clear boyish eyes. How could a woman like that sort of animal?

CHAPTER XVII

HAMILTON'S DISMISSAL.

There was talk of the approaching dissolution of the Ladies' Land League.[63] How devoutly Hamilton hailed the rumour! Now, at least, Morna had no reason to urge against his pressing his suit, and, his suit once gained, what delight he would have in sitting on that fool of an officer. He knew the hour Morna usually left Leeson-street for the office, and determined to surprise her early.

Morna and Marjory were alone at breakfast, laughing over Harston's likeness, which Morna found highly flattered, when Hamilton was announced.

---

63. The Ladies' Land League was dissolved on 8 August 1882. See Anna Parnell's *The Tale of a Great Sham*.

"Bring him up here, and let us have more coffee," said Morna.

Hamilton came up looking gravely expectant.

"You must pay the penalty of coming so early by joining us. What shall I offer you?"

"Nothing, Morna, thanks. I have breakfasted."

"At least you must have a cup of coffee," she said, instantly, handing him a cup.

He moved a chair towards the table, and began to stir his coffee leisurely; then looked up at Morna, brightly.

"When is this momentous dissolution to be?"

"I know nothing about it. We wanted it to take place at once on the release of the men, but it was pointed out to us then as impossible.[64] I confess I didn't look on it as much; I yet can't see why we could not have then handed in our report and retired into private life. Everyone is dissatisfied, and really our position is far from enviable," she sighed.

"Did you hear what Georgina Templeton said at a meeting in Sackville-street when the male heads came to discuss the crisis with the Russian generals and active Executive of the Ladies' Land League?"[65]

"No; how could I? That's your friend?"

"Of course. They were arranging for the formation of the Mansion House Committee, and one of the leaders—we never give names you know—was deliberating over some probabilities, when Georgina Templeton leant forward and looking at him in the gravest way, imaginable, said, just as coolly: "We'll undertake to recommend the committee to our country branches."[66] Of course everyone felt ready to fall off their chairs with laughter, but

---

64. 2 May 1882 – following the Kilmainham treaty, political prisoners including Parnell, Dillon, J. J. O'Kelly were released.
65. Georgina Templeton, modelled on Anna Parnell.
66. The Mansion House Fund was set up by Edmund Dwyer Gray, Lord Mayor of Dublin, 'in response to the Land League's call for assistance for the rural poor' (Groves 2009, pp. 131–2).

fancy the feelings of the men on that occasion."

"Whenever women have anything to do with men, Marjory, they generally manage, to use your favourite expression, to make them feel pretty bad at times," said Hamilton, seriously answering rather his own thought than her words.

Hamilton looked impressive, and Marjory knew enough of love to give him the opportunity she felt he desired. She withdrew on some indifferent pretext.

"Morna, the business for which you have been putting me off so long is surely over now. Am I to have any answer? May I hope?" he urged gently, looking into her eyes.

Her eyes met his gravely; she looked too sorry for his doom not to be written therein.

"Listen to me before you speak, Morna," he cried passionately, in his excitement, standing up and going towards the fireplace, where he stationed himself in front of her, grasping his coat-collar with both hands and speaking in repressed eagerness with his face illuminated with the strength of his own passion. "Before you answer me think—think, I beseech you, Morna, what you have been to me all these years; years of little pleasure and very much pain—I will ask you to believe in the pain, Morna. You alone have been the pleasure. You have told me often that it is something to have accomplished work, to have lived the life of a man, to have acquired a certain amount of knowledge, to perhaps have helped others to some knowledge. I tell you these things have been nothing to me since I knew you first, or only something inasmuch as they helped to make me worthier of you—of you, better than all these, than all life has hitherto offered me or is ever likely to offer me again. Oh, I see the protest on your face, and, Morna, you are wrong?" he urged, with something like a sob in his voice, as he held out both hands to her, "Will you not see that you will drive me to desperation if you send me from you hopelessly."

She did not take his hands, but bent forward, leaning her forehead against the hand which shielded her face and eyes from his, and he drew back, thrusting up his chin with an odd, quick, impetuous movement. and went on through his short, gasping breath.

"Yes, yes. I know what you are thinking: that I am a coward to say so; that that is only the hackneyed threat with which a man harasses the woman he pretends to love. I'll retract it if I can, because I would not have you think ill of me. But think, Morna, you have been all the world to me these years, more than the world, for that was never much to me. How will it be with me now, if you go out of my life, perhaps into another's, and leave me desolate? Is that no responsibility?"

"You are not fair to me, Herbert," she said, when his passionate fluency gave her time to speak. It was the first time she had called him by his Christian name, and the sound thrilled him like an unexpected caress. She looked up just then and saw by the wild radiance of his gaze that she had made a woman's mistake in trying to lessen his pain. "If I do not love you the way you ask me to love you, why need that fact thrust you from my life? If you cared for me it would be punishing you as well as me. I told you before that, that—"

"You did not tell me before what I think I can guess now," he interrupted, fiercely—"that you love or are interested in that officer."

"There is nothing in our friendship to justify a liberty of that nature," she cried, in cold restraint.

"There, I have angered you; you will hate me when you remember how unmanly I have been," he said despairingly, beginning to walk up and down the room in quick uneven strides.

"I thought it was a woman's privilege to jump at conclusions. If you are sorry for having hurt me so, I can certainly promise to forget it," she said gently.

"Sorry to have hurt you! Oh, my dear and dearest, my best one love, cannot you believe this at least, that it will be always the same for me? I think I am not exaggerating when I tell you that I have lived on your memory. You know me, Morna; I have not thought of other women. How can I tell you what I have felt and feel in language that will not appear false or hackneyed? So many men rave and rant and say they love women—so few understand it—still fewer feel it. Because they take a certain worthless pleasure in caressing a woman and turning her into a plaything; because they find her eyes very soft and bright; a certain sweep of cheek and throat adorably lovely, or a trick of voice or eyelid wonderful, they think they love. I know nothing about that kind of thing. I do not wish to appear subtle or more spiritual than I am; but if that were the sort of worship I have for you, Morna, it would not take long to satisfy the heart's hunger in change. I don't know if you are beautiful. I have not thought of it. Oh, if I were a poet! One must be a poet to express one's deep feelings. I can't. When I am near you or thinking of you, I seem to pass into a rarefied atmosphere, where the air is charged with finer spiritual electricity. I can think evil of no one when I remember your great goodness. O beloved—O my great-souled, large-hearted Morna! I am raving—I know I am; but be kind to me, give me some hope," he cried, flinging himself at her feet in a gesture of wild, impulsive entreaty, and catching her hands, which she had clasped before her eyes in a first impulse to shield herself from the sight of intolerable pain.

He knelt there, holding her hands from her pale, averted face; his own, one fierce glow—eyes, forehead, lips strained upward in a gaze of passionate pleading—self-forgetful, urgent, as though waiting to draw from her countenance agony or rapture.

"Will you go? It is best, believe me, since I cannot say what you want me to say."

She felt wretched, and looked at him through her tears in timid, beseeching sadness.

"Oh, no, not that answer. It is too late now. You should have said that long ago; now you have incurred responsibilities that would make it too great a wrong to throw me over now. You must accept them," he insisted, almost angrily.

She drew her hands from his and stood up, severe in her pale tranquillity.

"Why will you be so unjust to me? Was there ever an occasion on which you opened this subject that I did not do my best to make you see that it would end like this? At first I thought it was Marjory you loved, and I was glad, because I respect you more than any man I know. And then when I found that your hopes were not built on Marjory I was sorry, and tried to make you see how sorry I was, but I was proud, oh, yes, I was very proud, indeed, of the depth and earnestness of your devotion. Could I help it? If it was wrong, I heartily and wholly regret it. But you must not say that I've incurred any other responsibilities towards you, than those of sincerest gratitude and esteem, for I have not. I would not willingly have caused you a pang, but even to save you one, you would not have me give you a false assurance. I have no wish to marry."

"But you said, Morna—do you remember that night we walked to the office together?—that you would have time to think of me when your work was over and that you thought it not improbable that you might yet grow to care for me in that way. Did you give me no hope then? Think, be honest, Morna."

He was standing now facing her, with one hand resting on the table, the other hanging by his side, and his eyes looking straight into hers. He was as severe and earnest and calm now as she, calmer, because her mouth trembled slightly.

"I know—I know. I was wrong to speak as I did, but why will you remind me of it when you know I said it, and honestly meant it, because you seemed to think my life so necessary to you. Did you never make a mistake, even with the best intentions?"

This was changing their attitudes, and he was not slow to take advantage of it.

"Is it not the right thing to do when we have made a mistake to abide by the responsibilities our mistake involves?"

He spoke as coldly as a lawyer, but his whole heart was in his eyes, and his pulses were throbbing fearfully.

"You will make me think very differently of you if you insist on placing me in this cruel position," she said, losing her temper and flushing faintly. "Am I not doing my best to rectify my mistake? Have I not told you that I cannot marry you—that I have no idea of that life? How often have I said it to you? It is beautiful, if you will, but pray believe me when I tell you that I know a life more beautiful still. What can I say that will make you see that you are needlessly persecuting me?" she ended, catching her breath with a sob, and looking wildly around the room.

"Say that you love Mr. Dalrymple."

She thrust out both her hands in a gesture of petulant reproach; the flush on cheek and brow deepened in a sweep of wounded shame, and her clear, moist grey eyes looked tragic in their mute gaze. He caught her hands, thrilled by her look into a wave or revived tenderness.

"This is the second time I have gone against the nature of my reverence for you. Morna, forgive me. I see it now. But will you remember only that I have loved you, and that the value of my love has not been rendered base or worthless by past idle fancies, and that having now loved you, no other woman will fill the place you have reigned supreme in. I will go down to the grave having worshipped one sovereign, one saint. You shall live apart in my memory always near, always dear – dear above everything in life. I ask you to believe this. It is no idle protestation. Do you remember my errors or failings, beloved—for you will always be my beloved friend—or only remember them to contrast them with the greatness of my love. Whether you marry or choose a life of higher happiness, it shall be the same. For me it shall be as though a kindred soul had looked at me out of your eyes of holy grey, and after that I know my soul can know no change. Love has been best taught me by the knowledge of you, and if I have now to begin anew without that hope which has so long sustained me, in spite of the darkness and loneliness, I have been blessed past my merits, and the thought of that benediction will be my sustainment and reward. I had hoped for heaven as my home, but if I have missed heaven, I have gained much help and some of the whiteness of the passing angel. Good-by, it is good-by, but despite the change and distance you will find me ever ready to obey your lightest wish; you will find me faithful to my sovereign, and blest still by the grace of her smile."

He kissed her hand and left her thus.

(To be Continued – Commenced in No. 949.)

Vol. XXII. – No. 958.
Saturday, February 21, 1885: 325–327.

CHAPTER XVIII.

A SLIGHT MISUNDERSTANDING.

Left alone, Morna sat down with her head bent over her arm, and broke into sharp and shuddering sobs. To think that there was yet one man capable of such love; that the gift should have fallen to her who placed no hope or belief in such conquests, and have found her so unaccountably irresponsive. It was almost a dream, so beautiful and unselfish and perfect was it, and yet she had thrust it away from her forever after a hopeless effort to grasp it and rest satisfied in it, and she knew it would never be possible to bring it near her again. She knew, too, that Hamilton would have been very generous in their wedded life, that his nature was noble and chivalrous beyond that of ordinary manhood; that he would have helped her in whole-hearted earnestness in her charities, with her poor and ragged children; that if any man were capable of trying to make marriage ideal and a mutual blessing it would be Hamilton—and yet something strong within her broke out into absolute repugnance at the idea. She felt sure she had always been as averse to it as now. He had hinted otherwise, he even spoke of, of—the memory of his accusation stained her face anew in a swift scarlet wave, and she rose abruptly with a movement of proud denial and self-sustainment. She hastily dried her eyes as she heard Marjory's step.

"I heard Hamilton rush down stairs as if he was pursued by half a dozen fiends, and he dashed out of the house before I could overtake him and see what kind of face he wore," she cried, gaily, but the sight of Morna's red eyelids and sorrowful look brought her to a sudden pause. "You've been crying, Old Antiquity. What's the matter? Didn't he come to propose?"

"I wish he had fallen in love with you, Marge, before ever you met Harston; I'm sure you couldn't have helped caring for him, and he is so good and worthy that I'd have had no fear or pang in surrendering you to his care," said Morna, touching the little blonde head in a light caress.

"Then you've finally refused him. Well, Uncle Tom says you're too good for any man, and I'm greatly afraid you're egotistical enough to think the same, when you can send away such an eligible as Herbert Mercer. Why did you?"

"Because I have quite enough to do in minding you. If you marry there will be only the more reason for my taking care of you. I suspect I shall have to turn your housekeeper, and nurse, if there are any little ones by-and-by."

"Thank you, Morna," said Marjory, in part gravity. "You are proposing to come and play the part of Frou-Frou's clever sister when Frank and I are married, and end by discussing Frank with me in contrasting your goodness with my frivolity, till he follows the example of that prig—Frou-Frou's husband—and worships you.[67]

---

67. *Frou-Frou:* French comedy by Ludovic Halévy and Henri Meilhac. 'The story tells of an irresponsible young wife who invites her staid sister to live with her and her family so that she herself can flit about the town. She loses everyone›s affection and returns home to repent and to die'. Bordman, Gerald, and Thomas S. Hischak. «Frou-Frou.» *The Oxford Companion to American Theatre.* Oxford University Press. *Oxford Reference.* <https://www.oxfordreference.com/view/10.1093/acref/9780195169867.001.0001/acref-9780195169867-e-1124>. The analogy is proleptic.

You remember the night we went to see Bernhardt,[68] and I told you I'd never let you inside my door when I was married."

"But I think Frank would get on very well with a Frou-Frou who was contented with being simply charming and frivolous and merry. The rest needn't follow, you know."

"All the same, I don't believe in Dorothea Brookes[69] living in the houses of frivolous sisters; and I beg to exclude you from mine, except as a casual visitor. I got a lesson that night which I'm not likely to forget. Whenever Frank and I have an awful row I'll come home to you; then you'll only hear my version. But say, Morna, have you really made up your mind not to marry Hamilton?"

"Where's the use of speaking of it," said Morna, looking sadly away from the small, eager face.

"I never was so disappointed in all my life," cried Marjory, like every girl in love, strong in her belief that the condition of being engaged was the best of all possible conditions for the human race. "I thought I'd find you ready to read 'The Betrothed,'[70] or ready to burst frantically into 'Le Premier Baiser.'[71] In fact, I just came to gently revive your memory by playing it."

"Nothing can withstand my Nancy,"[72] said Morna, breaking into a smile.

"And do you really feel that but to see me is to love me—love but me, and love forever? Heigho, Harry! I wish I could feel sure

---

68. Sarah Bernhardt (1844–1923): Famous and popular French actress who performed the lead role in *Frou-Frou* at the Gaiety Theatre in Dublin on July 15th 1881. Advertisement in the *Freeman's Journal,* 12 July 1881, p. 4.
69. Dorothea Brooke: the idealistic young heroine of George Eliot's *Middlemarch* (1871–2).
70. Alessandro Manzoni, *I Promessi Sposi:* published in1840 and then in English as *The Betrothed* in 1844.
71. 'Le Premier Baiser': possibly a reference to a composition by French composer Georges Lamothe in 1868.
72. A reference to 'Ae Fond Kiss' by Robert Burns: 'I'll ne'er blame my partial fancy,/Naithing could resist my Nancy;/But to see her was to love her;/Love but her, and love forever. https://www.poetryfoundation.org/poems/43798/ae-fond-kiss

that Frank will love me forever."

Morna looked gravely into the transiently sad eyes with the shadow of pathos lingering round their long lashes.

"Do you doubt him really, Marjory?"

She herself did, but kept silent about her fear.

"Is it doubt poor Frank? I don't know whether I do or not. I don't like to think about it till I see him. I suppose he has a string of girls on hand in Dublin now. You know he is like one of Ouida's young men.[73] He likes to have a lot of girls rowing him about in boats, and metaphorically crowning him with flowers, sending him pocket-books, gold pencils, cigar-cases, and those sort of things. It's his way; he can't help liking flattery and adulation. I doubt if he could be content with knowing a girl whom he couldn't call by some pet name, and really there is no harm in him, as long as he likes me best I'm not going to quarrel about such humbug."

"I question if you are right, child, in permitting your affianced husband such an unusual latitude," said Morna severely.

"What! Would you expect me to fling myself on his breast like a second edition of Mrs. Micawber?"[74] If you were anywhere knocking around, I guess he'd look over my drooping head appealingly, and cry to you, in an intense undertone, 'Morna, is there anything you can suggest to me that would induce her by any possibility to desert me?' Look at me! Don't I flirt with Brecknock and Power? And that doesn't make me any the less fond of Frank. I can't bear lovers to be exacting, though they may be as jealous as they like; that's all the more fun. Wait till you see how we'll quarrel to-morrow."

"Don't say anything too bitter, Marge. It's a sad mistake, in the long run."

Morna heartily wished her sister out of the whole thing, but if that was not to be, she hated the idea of their quarrelling.

---

73. Ouida: Pen-name of popular novelist and short story writer, Marie Louise de la Ramée (1839–1908).

74. Mrs Micawber: devoted wife in Charles Dickens' *David Copperfield* (1850).

"Oh, I have my tactics, like Sir Garnet Wolseley, or any other general.[75] Do you remember the way Kate enticed that cat she wanted to punish when it ran away with the cold chicken? I never forgot the deceitful way she coaxed it, pretending she wanted to caress it, and when she had her hand on its coat produced the poker from behind her back. That's the way I'll act. You know he must be punished; so I'll receive him in an attitude of gentle expectancy and tranquillity. That will induce him to launch out in greater assurance, and then I'll pour all the vials of my wrath down on his head, in the thundering Juno fashion, when I've properly horrified and subdued and frightened him with the virulence of my tongue, I'll look at him with my large frank eyes, and I'll say 'Frank,' just like that, in the tone and look which novelists tell us convey unutterable things; and then, and then"—

She fluttered, in her bird-like aimless way, to the piano, where she sat poised, just like a bird stopping before it takes to flight again, and struck into "*Undi si ben,*" bending forward prettily to catch the notes.[76] Her playing drowned the sounds below, and even the knock outside before the door was opened by Denzil.

"Don't stir," he said, smiling. "You look so quaint that it wouldn't be a pity to break the picture, would it not, Miss Maurice? he asked, holding out his hand to Morna.

Marjory happened to look up at one, and saw what startled her into a new belief. Denzil's colour had deepened into a blush as his eyes met Morna's, and she saw an answering red wave faintly into Morna's pale cheeks, while her calm, grey eyes seemed darker and

---

75. Sir Garnet Wolseley: Dublin-born Anglo-Irish army officer who rose through the ranks, particularly via his involvement in various colonial projects. He did not support the Irish Nationalist cause. Beckett, Ian F. W. 'Wolseley, Garnet Joseph, first Viscount Wolseley (1833–1913), army officer.' *Oxford Dictionary of National Biography.* Oxford University Press. <https://www.oxforddnb.com/view/10.1093/ref:odnb/9780198614128.001.0001/odnb-9780198614128-e-36995>
76. Undi si ben: a reference to the famous quartet from Guiseppe Verdi's *Rigoletto* (1851), 'Un dì, se ben rammentomi', evoking Marjory's emotional state.

more radiant, unless the shadow of the deep brown lashes had something to do with it. Marjory wondered, and could believe it nothing but a revelation. She laughed aloud in delight at her discovery, and rushed out of the room to execute downstairs what she called a war-dance on the strength of it.

Denzil lifted his eyebrows inquiringly, and turned from looking after her in brief astonishment back to Morna's face.

"What is the matter with her to-day?"

"If I know," laughed Morna, with a little foreign gesture of head and hands. "She is simply in very good spirits."

"Oh, I see. Mr. Frank Harston is coming back," he said, seating himself opposite her, and looking at her with his grave, large gaze.

That old effectiveness I alluded when first introducing him was now very apparent; that certain liquid radiance in the eyes.

He saw that there still lingered signs of weeping round her eyes, and this evidence of human trouble brought her somewhat out of the ideal remoteness which held her aloof from him. He looked vaguely round the room, as though in search of some tangible justification of her grief, and finding none his eyes travelled back to that sweet, pale face in wistful questioning. He could not resist the impulse to put it into words.

"Something has grieved you; am I in the way now? If so I will return when you are not disturbed. But tell me am I asking too much when I ask you if I can be of any use," he urged helplessly.

His words produced an electrical effect on Morna and he saw it with an amazement. The memory of Hamilton's accusation swept down upon her in a flood of shame. Her face was stained in crimson, her eyelids dropped and he could see that her hands shook.

"There has occurred nothing personally to grieve me," she said, not looking at him. "Thanks for wishing to help me; you are kind, and you will not think me rude, will you? if I ask you to excuse me now. I have been detained beyond my hour for going to the office and now that we are coming near the end of our work, you have no idea how much there is to be done." She rose and bent her eyes on her watch to avoid meeting the earnest gaze she felt fixed on her face.

The fact that she was avoiding his eyes pierced him with a sense of keen disappointment. It was not her way to deal in uncandid subterfuges, and could it mean? He rose too and stood looking at her mournfully.

"When will you be free, Miss Maurice?" She started back slightly. The question reminded of Hamilton, and thrilled her with a sudden pang. She just looked at him once with her wide sincere eyes; looked at him gravely with proud repression.

"I hardly understand. If you mean from the office; the Ladies' Land League is nearing its dissolution. Good morning. If you are not in a hurry perhaps Marjory will play for you."

CHAPTER XIX

A WRONG INFERENCE.

During the past six months Denzil had become a constant visitor at Maurices. Having once acknowledged to himself the wonderful attraction Morna had for him, he resolved to give free scope to the feeling without stopping to analyse if it were love or merely a sentiment he felt. Morna met him frankly, always looked glad to see him, and each time he grew to imagine she was more beautiful and exquisitely gracious than she had appeared even on the last occasion. If he remained away from her an entire week to test the strength of his feeling against which he felt himself powerless to struggle, he found nothing could stay the yearning hunger just to look into those lustrous grey eyes, and the look once taken, he felt serener, less passion-tossed, and as if he had taken a long draft of cool, pure water in a desert. It was extraordinary the influence this girl, surrounded by so much that was objectionable to him, exercised over him, and how quietly he bent to it. Of course, he was not long without discovering in Herbert Mercer Hamilton a rival, and not a rival to be thought of lightly either. While Hamilton remained in prison it was hard to judge the danger accurately. Sometimes he used to think that Morna's tranquil, matronly benignity wedded to her sweet smile and grave graciousness was the result of an assured position which enabled her to regard other men as a large-minded young wife would who walked apart and yet attracted them into the circle of her goodness, strong in her own truth and in her husband's belief in her. Under the spell of this conviction, he would writhe in a despairing sense of remoteness from her and the heavy weight of silence it imposed upon him. But it was scarcely jealousy he felt towards Hamilton. He recognised the man's ability and a certain nobleness of demeanour which impressed him vaguely. Then, too, his love for Morna stood him in place of a fixed religious belief, and, as such, excluded jealousy. If Morna really married Hamilton he sometimes doubted if he would be capable of hating Hamilton, as he knew in the natural course of events he was bound to hate him. He could even fancy himself readily admitting that he was a very good fellow, and almost worthy of Morna. Certainly, he had not met any man more capable of assuring her happiness, and he recognised the man as vastly his own intellectual superior. Then there was the counter conviction that Morna loved no man, but met them all shielded in that impenetrable nun-like impersonality of hers, and he hardly knew which to prefer. Neither filled him with joy, but left him equally chilled with the impotence of his own personality to strike the note of unison on hers. Thus, up to the time of Hamilton's release, when he had attended Land League meetings, and listened to any of the popular orators, who found themselves in a position to address the citizens in or about Dublin, he did his best to grasp at the causes and effects of the Land League doctrines; sent anonymously a large subscription to the Ladies' organisation, studied the rules of the movement, the debates across the water, listened attentively to Morna's theories, greatly wondered at some of them, but respected even the wildest. He was a frequent visitor at Power's lodgings and drank in eagerly anything that eccentric individual had to say of the Maurices; attended Mass regularly in Gardiner-street because Morna went there every Sunday, found the music vaguely soothing and the glimpses he got of Morna's side-face in its prayerful stillness with the lights touching the pale cheek into transient warmth and bringing out the strong contrast of her dark hair above the neck, and growing low on her broad brow, and the wide sweep of long dark lashes cutting their way under the drooping eyelids, ineffably beautiful. If her attendance at Mass could give him such a picture, he was willing that she should attend it all her life, provided she would only give him the chance of accompanying her. He remembered intimately the names of everyone, man and woman, connected with the Land League, could quote from some of their orators, and had to bear with much quizzing at the United Service Club where Brecknock had made known some of his amazing exploits. When Hamilton came out of Kilmainham he was careful to treat him, whenever they met in Leeson-street, to a marked courtesy, to which the other responded somewhat coldly.

But this sudden strangeness of behaviour in a woman so free from feminine capriciousness filled him with astonishment and pain. He could account for it in no other way but that she had finally accepted Hamilton, and as her future husband he had objected to the kindness with which another lover had been received. It seemed absurd and unjust to object to anything Morna thought right, and had it fallen to his lot to be trusted with that great gift of her love, he did not think he would begrudge another poor devil the futile pain of witnessing it and drawing what comfort he could from her presence. As for doubting Morna or thinking she might not be trusted with a universe of men—jealousy of such a nature as hers was almost a slight on the very exquisiteness of that nature. He stood watching her turn up the street from the window in a kind of dull, dreary pain, and felt then that he would have been worthier of her than Hamilton, since his love, because of its very immovable faith, must be the broader and deeper. Marjory found him thus with his hands joined behind and his forehead pressed against the glass.

"Really," thought that young lady, "Morna surpasses my comprehension altogether. Is she going to be a nun or an old maid when she can reject one suitor and snub another—one learned, the other a gentleman by birth? I'm afraid, Mr. Dalrymple," she said aloud, "that my magnificent sister is not in what we might call quite an amiable mood to-day. I think she is worried about some letters, and I know she and Mr. Hamilton did not part the best friends this morning."

Marjory thought this news would soothe and charm Denzil, instead of which it only confirmed him in his belief that there had been a lover's quarrel on his account. He made no answer, but looked gloomier and sadder than Marjory had thought him capable of looking, as he turned to walk up and down the room. He stopped suddenly in front of her when she was puzzling her brains for the right thing to say.

"Have you heard your sister say anything that would lead you to imagine that she would prefer my visits here to cease?"

"No. Why should she say such a thing as that? It is very absurd to take that idea into your head, Mr. Dalrymple, because Morna is a little irritable to-day. She is never irritable except then she comes home tired from the office. Oh! Morna is the best girl in the world; she is perfect, and she is so good that I don't like to think of her goodness, it is so beyond me and all that, but since the Land League started I have known my sister, Morna, to come down from her angelic pedestal on a few occasions, and solace me greatly by proving, that she is at least capable of something like human infirmity, by an occasional sarcasm very neatly delivered, and faith not quite unworthy of myself, and by certain little cross and irritable ways when she is overworked."

"Why, in heaven's name, should she be permitted to overwork

herself? When she came home to dinner on last Wednesday, her face was quite white and drawn, and her eyes as languid as if she hadn't slept for nights," he cried warmly. "It is not right, and, Miss Marjory, you should be very tender to her when she is so tired; it is hard to expect a woman's delicate nerves not to break down under such a strain, and I, who don't profess to be a cross-grained or bad-tempered fellow, if I came home worried and half-dead with fatigue, I can tell you I'd kick up the devil of a row. If I were Mr. Maurice I'd fight against your sister killing herself by inches as she is; he complained to me that she refused to go anywhere this summer, and ask yourself is she not badly in need of rest and change?"

"She is; I know she is. Uncle Tom does not know, but she is really ill. Nothing agrees with her, and, indeed, she hardly eats anything. Very often instead of dining when she comes home, she goes up to her room and lies down for an hour or so, and she does not fall asleep as you or I would if we were tired; it is more like a dead prostration of all her energies. She looks quite like a corpse, and her hands are shudderingly cold if you touch them."

"And in the name of all that is wonderful is there no doctor in this city of yours that she should be left like that?" he cried, jumping up impetuously. "Have you no influence over her? Has Mr. Hamilton none? One would think it was his interest and duty at least to shield her from her own imprudence and folly."

"Oh, I don't see what special reason Mr. Hamilton has to interfere any more than the rest of her friends," said Marjory, meaningly. "She doesn't listen to me."

Denzil believed Marjory had been kept in ignorance of Morna's position towards Hamilton; such an evidence of reticence between sisters astonished him, but he said nothing, determining within himself to call on Hamilton. He took up Harston's likeness which Marjory had left on the table and began to examine it casually. He felt a strong dislike for the face.

"That's Frank," said Marjory, looking over his shoulder at it with a glad, bright look.

"Yes; it is a good likeness," said Denzil, raising his eyes from it and abruptly fixing them on the small, excited face beside him, the steady penetration of his glance bringing into it a delicate flush. "Poor child," he thought in that kindly, protective tenderness for all women some men cannot escape. The mere fact of finding himself near a girl gave him the consciousness of vague responsibility. "What a horrible pity she should have selected a little cad like this Harston fellow to give him that flattering girl's heart of hers. There is nothing for her now but to abide by the consequences, which, something tells me, will be sad for her. Even poor Brecknock, with all his foolish way of talking of girls, would have made her not a bad husband in the long run. That little face poised so perilously between sunshine and shadow, with pathos lying so near the laughter, would have brought out all the best of him, and would have turned him into a tender sort of fellow, for he is a gentleman with all a gentleman's honour and truth. But this Harston is only a mean-looking cad, with his false mouth and fatuous smile."

"We are going to have torpedo practising next Thursday outside the harbour. Brecknock and I will expect you and Mr. Maurice on the 'Adversary,'" he said, smiling.

Vol. XXII. – No. 959.
Saturday, February 28, 1885: 347–349.

CHAPTER XX

A TALK IN THE OFFICE.

The next day was the eve of the opening of the Exhibition.[77] Marjory, not certain of the hour Frank would arrive, went down to the office, where she remained till dinner-time. She sat

---

77. The exhibition opened on the 15th August 1882.

in the outer room, in her gayest, maddest mood, writing letters for Georgina Templeton, whose secretary she called herself, and holding an uninterrupted conversation with her friend at the same time.

"Will you come to the rehearsal of the concert tonight, Georgina? I'm going to make Frank come. It'll be some value."

"Where's the use? We'll see it tomorrow, besides I'm afraid I shall have far too much to do for such frivolous nonsense. Did you hear we're going to put up Arabi's flag as soon as the procession begins?[78] Your seat is on the second row, beside Tilly Frankenson and Mrs. Carton."

"I'd stay to help in the preparations tonight only I expect Frank Harston."

"When is that marriage coming off?"

Marjory flushed a little, and said in a lower voice:

"Who can ever answer a question like that? Why don't you fall in love, Georgy, and give me good example?"

"You see you mightn't follow it, and I'd have made a fool of myself for nothing. But I'm of the same opinion as that fellow who wrote *Virginibus Puerisque*.[79] I never saw or read of any man worth falling in love with except perhaps Leonardo da Vinci; in my

---

78. Arabi: 'Urabi ['Arabi], Ahmad Muhammad [Aḥmad Muḥammad 'Urabī; known as Arabi Pasha] (1841–1911), army officer and politician in Egypt who led a revolt that was suppressed by the British'. Rogan, Eugene. "'Urabi ['Arabi], Ahmad Muhammad [Aḥmad Muḥammad 'Urabī; known as Arabi Pasha] (1841–1911), army officer and politician in Egypt." *Oxford Dictionary of National Biography.* 23 Sep. 2004. https://www.oxforddnb.com/view/10.1093/ref:odnb/9780198614128.001.0001/odnb-9780198614128-e-53767.

   Connections between Irish nationalism and Arabi's revolt were made by Lady Augusta Gregory in her article, 'Arabi and his household' in *The Times* 23 October 1882. See O'Cinnéide 2016, pp. 25–38.

79. Robert Louis Stevenson, a writer much admired by Lynch. It is unclear here whether Georgina Templeton is referring to the essay, 'Virginibus Puerisque', published in 1876 or a collection of essays by Stevenson published under the same title in 1881.

credulous moods I'm inclined to add the Admirable Crichton[80] or the Chevalier Lauzun as most fascinating."[81]

"What! not even Hilarion?"[82]

"Bosh! Hilarion was a most reprehensible young man to mention nothing of exaggeration. 'These things do sometimes die, I believe,' when he saw the girl he had pretended to love a ghastly corpse. There is a letter from Dunphy, of Belmullet, to be answered. Tell him I have not received the instructions he refers to, and that the case in under inquiry."

"And don't you find any of our own men as interesting as Leonardo da Vinci? asked Marjory, pausing before addressing an envelope.

"I certainly cannot say I was ever particularly fascinated by any Irishman or Englishman I read of or saw. I find them a very ordinary and uninteresting collection of individuals. If you've written that letter I want you to direct the secretary of the Lodore Branch—post town, Cardoon, Galway—to send us all the particulars of the

---

80. Admirable Crichton: Crichton, Admirable (James Crichton) (1560–85) A Scottish scholar, poet, and linguist who travelled in France and Italy, served in the French army, and died in a brawl in Mantua. His career was described by Sir Thomas Urquhart in his writings in praise of the Scots nation *The Discoverie of a Most Exquisite Jewel* (1652) and the Admirable Crichton developed a reputation as a perfect man with many varied talents. Delahunty, Andrew, and Sheila Dignen. "Crichton, Admirable". *A Dictionary of Reference and Allusion.* Oxford University Press. Oxford Reference. <https://www.oxfordreference.com/view/10.1093/acref/9780199567454.001.0001/acref-9780199567454-e-491>.
81. Chevalier Lauzun: Armand Louis de Gontaut Lauzun (1747–1793) – another historical figure and example of heroic masculinity, who served in the French Guards and is associated with the American Revolution. Britannica, T. Editors of Encyclopaedia. 'Armand-Louis de Gontaut, duke de Biron'. *Encyclopedia Britannica,* December 27, 2021. https://www.britannica.com/biography/Armand-Louis-de-Gontaut-duc-de-Biron.
82. Hilarion: The dashingly handsome young nobleman, Count d'Acugna, and hero of Sydney Owenson's *The Missionary: An Indian Tale (1811).* Taking on the saint's name Hilarion, having renounced his privilege to become a monk and missionary in India, he proves himself less than heroic in his treatment of Luxima, an Indian prophetess.

Murphy eviction case. They apply for a grant of five pounds, and I know nothing yet of the circumstances under which they were evicted."

"Haven't you really met a handsome Irishman?" persisted Marjory.

"No. That landlord is a ruffian."

"Don't you find Frank handsome?"

"Who? Harston? Heavens! no. He is the image of an Italian mountebank, Miss Lennon, haven't you these Ruston tenants on hands! This letter refers to the Widow Murtagh; this other is about that man who did not shoot the bailiff, but gave every proof of cherishing such intentions. Please bring it to Miss Frankenson as it belongs to the legal department."

She was too busy to notice the effect of her cruel truthfulness on poor Marjory and went on, between the pauses of business:

"I've taken great stock of men in public assemblies, at parties, in churches and at meetings and I find them all a dead level of monotony and coarseness. There is more variety in ten women's faces than in a hundred men's. As for their costumes—they are certainly neither airy nor graceful."

"Am I to tell Denis Longestaffe of Ennis that his case has been placed before the Mansion House Committee? And will you never marry, Georgy?"

"Very probably I shall if any sufficiently eligible party presents himself. I can't say of course; but this I know that I am not ever likely to be in love with my husband, and if he doesn't insist on me finding him charming or particularly interesting it is quite possible that I shall get on with him no worse than the generality of wives. Those papers had better be left aside for the Russian generals to-night. I've quite enough with these."

"Here, Martin, put those with the parcels; there are the addresses. 'Pon my word, Georgy, I'm glad I haven't your views; they are very sad ones."

"Not a bit sad when you're used to them; they're even quite racy."

"Then you are likely to marry the first man who asks you?"

"Oh, dear, no. Why should I? He might be deformed, and I'm not a Maggie Tulliver, I assure you; or he might be a drunkard."[83]

"That would be much worse."

"Well, perhaps worse. You'd feel bad, no doubt, the first time you saw him reeling home with a glassy, vacant stare and an insane grin, to say nothing of worse consequences. Then he might have an unpleasant way of pronouncing certain words. For instance, I couldn't stand a man who would say juke for duke, or p'lice or polis for police. And he might not be rich, which would assuredly be the worst possibility of all."

Marjory laughed, and bent to look among some papers, when Georgina whispered:

"Here comes Bunthorne; probably your ideal of Hilarion."[84]

Marjory looked up, and her face was bathed in a delicate light as she saw Frank Harston smiling blandly.

"There was a gleam of sunshine, it was Hilarion," laughed Georgina, sarcastically.[85]

"I can't endure that fellow; I wish she'd give him up," said a lady Land Leaguer as Marjory disappeared with her lover.

"Poor child! I suspect he'll be giving her up soon enough. Did you hear about that girl down in Wicklow he is after? Plain-looking, I believe, but a great heiress. They say she'll marry him, but why I can't tell; for I know she is of much better family than he, and all her people are rich, too."

"The little one doesn't know about it, of course—she's as bright as ever?"

---

83. Maggie Tulliver: the tragic heroine of George Eliot's *Mill on the Floss* (1860).
84. Reginald Bunthorne: 'The principal male character in Gilbert and Sullivan's opera *Patience*, a 'fleshly poet', in whose person the Aesthetic Movement of the 1880s was caricatured'. ("Bunthorne, Reginald". *Oxford Reference*. https://www.oxfordreference.com/view/10.1093/oi/authority.20110803095535625).
85. Georgina's sarcastic characterisation of Frank Harston as Hilarion anticipates Marjory's fate.

"Oh, she'll be bright to the end. But don't you see she's got thinner and paler? Once or twice I noticed her looking as sad as anyone could look."

"You think she suspects it?"

"Oh, no, not at all. Women never do suspect things like that till it comes on them like a blow. Marjory is one of those little fools that would fly at you if you suggested the idea, and will only be got to believe in that fellow's falseness when she sees his marriage with another woman in the newspaper."

"Do you know if the report has reached Miss Maurice?"

"I daresay not," said Miss Templeton. "But I fancy she never favoured his suit. I want Marjory to leave that fellow and come down this evening and give us a representation of Kilmainham and the House of Commons, particularly a speech of Mark Luke's, before we break up, but she won't."

CHAPTER XXI

A LOVER'S QUARREL.

It did not take long for Harston to make his peace with Marjory, and by the time they had reached Leeson-street he had fairly succeeded in persuading her that he had been treated badly enough by her, and that he was a right good fellow to pass it over so lightly. He referred pathetically to the brutality of fate, which ordained that his holiday by her side should be cut short by that governor of his, in order that he might spend some time down in Wicklow, a place he loathed. Marjory pouted a little on the mention of Wicklow, and hinted darkly at the existence of Miss Trediger. Of course, this brought from Harston a rush of passionate protestations, of hatred and contempt of Miss Trediger, of undying fidelity to his Irish Juliet, &c.

"And you really think you will always love me best, Frank, in spite of your father's influence, and all this worry?" she asked when they were in the parlour.

"Love you best, darling? Why, who in the world is like my own Marge? I should think so, pet," he said, encircling her with his arms.

"Yes, but I sometimes cannot help doubting you. My uncle seems to think you don't really care for me," she said, wistfully.

"Oh, indeed. What has your uncle been saying about me, pray!" he sneered.

The sneer angered her justly, and she said, withdrawing herself from his embrace:

"Only this, that he is dissatisfied with our engagement, and thinks you are not behaving well to me."

"I hate that uncle of yours, a meddlesome old woman, that's what he is," cried Harston, furiously.

This news that Mr. Maurice was criticising him thrilled him with fear. It was just possible that things might turn out disagreeable by and by with such visions of an infuriated uncle in the background.

"You have no right to speak in that way, Frank, of my uncle," retorted Marjory, with darkly-brilliant eyes and set lips. "He is very good, he has been very good to me always, and he has never once interfered with you."

"Isn't he interfering with me now, when he tries to turn you against me in my absence?" asked Harston, pettishly.

"No, he never tried to turn me against you. He said you were treating me badly and that he'd prefer the thing to end at once; and what he said was right. I had better give you up at once. It is no use; you'll only go away and make me suffer more pain."

There was a little break in her voice which touched Harston's worthless tenderness. He jumped up and was by her side pressing his cheek against her shoulder.

"Marjory, you are very hard on me, and make me say lots of things I don't mean and am sorry for as soon as said. Why do you speak of giving me up? You know you couldn't give me up; neither of us now could do that. Tell me your uncle hasn't made you love me less, and I won't mind what he said of me. Tell me, darling. You won't make me wretched by speaking again of giving me up, unless you like to give me up in this way," he added, looking into her eyes as he caught her lightly into his arms and kissed her. "That is the only kind of giving up lovers should understand."

"I forgive you, Frank," she said, as soon as he had released her, "but you really must not speak like that again of my uncle. If he were like your father, anxious to separate me on the question of expediency, you would have reason to feel harshly towards him; but I have that cause, and I didn't call your father a meddlesome old woman, though I candidly confess I loathe him."

"Oh, come now, Marge, my poor father is a very good sort of governor in his way. It is because he is anxious about me that he goes on like that. I believe this nonsense with those women down in Sackville-street will soon be at an end. I'm very glad of it, Marge, and only wish you had never mixed yourself up with anything so disreputable."

"You know, Frank, that I don't like you to speak that way of the Ladies' Land League, and I won't have it. Are you going out to Roiville to see the Handcocks?"

"I suppose I'll have to. Are you and Evy great friends yet?"

"No; Uncle Tom told me to give her up, and I was very glad. We went to see the Centaur and she behaved very badly on board."

"Do you mean to tell me, Marjory, that you and she visited the Centaur alone?"

"Yes," she answered, fiercely.

"You want somebody constantly at your heels to keep you from going to the devil headlong," he ended, walking up and down with his face set in cold disapproval.

Marjory chafed under his brutal anger, and the light in her eyes burnt and dried up the tears which had gathered in them. She sat on the sofa with her head flung proudly backward in her resolution not to regret her frankness, two red spots deeply staining her cheeks, and her unseeing eyes gazing fiercely down the room. She knew his attack was unjustifiable and unloverlike, and she felt a mad impulse to fling her arms up in the air and cry aloud. But she sat there silently, and at last he paused before her and looked at her critically.

"Well, at least there is some comfort in the notion that your uncle has put an end to these charming expeditions."

"I don't understand you, Mr. Harston. I think you had better leave me. No one has used such language to me as you did now. My uncle was angry, but at least he knew how to conduct himself as a gentleman. Good-by. I'm sorry I ever had anything to do with you. I used to think you so different, but now I see I have been a fool. You needn't come to see me again ever," she ended, petulantly, in childish terror of the sobs she felt rising to her throat. "Go away. I hate you, and I'm very glad I've been flirting with Mr. Brecknock while you were away."

This was a bit of bravado to keep off the tragic element, and it helped her to a short, hysterical laugh.

"Oh, indeed," sneered Harston, from the door, with a look of withering contempt. "That's the fellow you all believe a naval officer. Some gunner, probably. Is he your typical gentleman? A coarse, red-faced fellow."

"He is not coarse. He's a gentleman, what you are not, since he would never speak that way of any one, and he at least knows how to address a woman. If you weren't so ignorant, you'd know he is first lieutenant on the Adversary. There, go away, do," she cried, stamping her foot.

Poor Marjory, for a heroine—why?—was woefully deficient in dignity in the quarrel, this she felt herself with much shame and when left alone did throw up her arms, and fall down a mere fragile mass against the sofa, her form shaken with convulsive sobs, which rose in a choking swell in the fair, slender throat. She grasped it between her hands and lay there sobbing in pathetic forlornness. If Frank would only come back again, and give her the chance of saying something better, behaving with more dignity. What could he think her now but a silly shrew, and yet surely she had received provocation enough to justify anything she might have said? then came the maddening idea that she had let him off too lightly. He had spoken abominably, and nothing could excuse him; she had given him his dismissal for the present, but, of course, by-and-by when her anger was cooled down sufficiently and he had made ample atonement she would forgive him. After all the real quarrel had begun at his anger with her for having placed herself in a false position. But what if he should not return? What if he should not seek to make amends and soothe her wounded pride, but hold aloof and coldly accept his dismissal?. Oh, then he could not love her, and she would feel death a pleasant release to life under circumstances so unendurable. While she was sobbing and arguing in her passionate incoherence Harston was met by Mr. Maurice on the stairs and quickly motioned into the dining-room.

"I learnt from Marjory that you were to be here this evening, and have been waiting to speak to you, Mr. Harston," cried Mr. Maurice, pointing to a seat and fixing him with a cold, steady stare.

Frank felt horribly uncomfortable, but sat down and laughed audaciously as he crossed his legs and pulled at a minute moustache.

"Gad it's not often a frivolous chap like me is in request in such staid company as yours, Mr. Maurice. I hope you don't want to put me through my paces on the question of figures and stocks. I've the devil of a head in those matters."

"Young man, I wish to be favoured with none of your impertinent nonsense," interrupted Mr. Maurice, sternly. "I have not hitherto shown you that I consider you capable of moderately serious conversation, notwithstanding your supposed brilliant qualifications. I've seen none of them; I wish to see none of them, possibly because I'm only too willing to take them on trust to be spared the infliction of discovering them for myself. To tell you the truth, Mr. Harston, I'd be glad enough if I had never laid my eyes on you, but as you are here I want to know now what are you going to do."

This question was unmistakable, and certainly the prelude was uncompromising. Harston bit his lip, looked coldly fierce and contemptuous, and uncrossed his legs.

"If you will be good enough to be more explicit, Mr. Maurice, I shall perhaps be able to answer you. You have confined yourself chiefly to your dislike of me."

"You understand me well enough, sir. I refer to this engagement or whatever you choose to call it that exists between you and my niece," cried Mr. Maurice, standing up with his clenched hand resting on the table.

"It is kind of you to oblige me with this explanation; I will now oblige you with another, Mr. Maurice," said Harston, rising with his jaunty air and buttoning up his outer coat. "Your niece has done me the honour to dismiss me just now. Since you are frank enough to declare your sentiments in that unmistakable language which does you credit, it will probably afford you much satisfaction to learn of my dismissal, and now perhaps you'll extend your goodness so far as to spare me any comments."

"It would give me some satisfaction to extend it so far as to throw you out of the window," roared the elder man in black rage. "As it is, I'll content myself with telling you that I'm heartily glad to see the girl has common sense enough to pitch you to the devil without seeking to know the why or the wherefore."

He saw Harston's dark, contemptuous smile, and had much to do to restrain himself from clutching his throat, but let him leave the room without another word.

It was past the usual hour when Morna returned to dinner. Her uncle met her in the hall and touched her shoulder with his first finger, as was his habit, nodding his head as he looked upstairs.

"Go up and bring her down to dinner. I dare say she is crying herself sick now that she has sent that insufferable little cad about his business."

"Harston! Is it possible? Poor Marge! But how do you know that it means anything more than their other quarrels?" asked Morna, placing her hat and gloves on the hall-stand and looking at her uncle uneasily.

"Oh, I had him in here all to myself, and he very kindly treated me to a little of his insolence," said her uncle, thrusting his hands into his trouser-pockets and looking down sideways.

"Is it a case of his or her withdrawing?" Morna asked, anxiously.

"Oh, of course he says she has dismissed him. He couldn't well say otherwise to me, you know. We know very well what that means, that he's been behaving badly and got her to quarrel with him. Anyway, I'm glad she's out of it, and go up to her and tell her so. That's the best sort of comfort you can give her till her grief wears itself out. I'm glad of all this excitement about the Exhibition. She is astonishingly mercurial, and we'll take care to give her plenty of amusement for the next month or so."

"My poor child," cried Morna, moving upstairs.

That week Harston went down to Wicklow. He had not quite made up his mind whether he would let the matter rest conveniently there or seek to renew relationship with Marjory, and thought it best to leave his definite course of action still a matter of speculation. After all, the final rupture must come some day, since he had made up his mind to thrust his brilliant career into the Trediger channel with the kindly intentions of helping an unambitious young lady to get through her fortune, and both his father and his friend Neville solemnly asseverated their belief in his speedy success.

Mr. Maurice was right in believing that the excitement would act as a powerful sedative to Marjory's sorrow. At night she would sometimes waken suddenly and rise in bed with a quick, nervous shudder, conscious of some heavy oppression, sick with the sense of isolation and forlorness [sic]. At such times of dark misery and loneliness she would stretch out her arms pitifully to the beloved image of Frank, recalling his caresses with fond words, each feature and gesture in passionate bitterness, and morbidly deepening the intensity of privation. But during the day, when surrounded with others, she was as bright and merry as ever, and Brecknock never found her so charming and witty as the day of the torpedo practising when she and her uncle came on board the Adversity [sic].

Evelyn Handcock was there, bland and simpering as ever. She greeted Marjory and her uncle warmly, and was astonished at her reception. Mr. Maurice stared at her coldly, gathered his niece more closely on his arm, and responded curtly to her salutation. Marjory blushed, and gave her a mute, imploring look. But the astonishment was turned into a sense of personal wrong when the Roiville flirt found that her two best friends on the Adversary were eagerly, specially attentive to Marjory. It is true Denzil was more civil to her than Brecknock was, but the merest observation soon drew even Denzil from her side when the speaker was Marjory.

"So you've overcome your first distaste for midnight drives on outside cars, for trades-people and women-speakers?" she sneered.

"If you are referring to the Miss Maurices, I am proud to say that I have overcome every prejudice in their regard, with which I unfortunately started," he said calmly.

"That's so very charming; it's quite wonderful, indeed. I'm thinking of turning woman's righter."

"Don't. It wouldn't suit you," he rejoined with a subtle smile.

Evelyn was furious, and looked over at Marjory, who was then laughing excitedly, while Brecknock was bending down to say something to her with a delighted face. He had the air of a privileged lover, and Evelyn bit her lips angrily.

(To be Continued – Commenced in No. 949.)

CHAPTER XXII.

DENZIL'S VISIT TO HAMILTON.

Denzil was greeted on his entrance to the United Service Club the evening of the Exhibition with a rush of sarcastic comments on the procession and concert.

"I hear you helped the Lord Mayor to open the performance," sneered one, "and that you stood beside the uncrowned king at the unveiling of the memorial to hold his hat and handkerchief and all that sort of thing."

"I didn't see the unveiling of the statue," said Denzil, quietly. "I saw the procession from a window at the top of Sackville-street. I thought it a fine National business."

"Were you situated anywhere near these irrepressible females in Sackville-street?"

"Yes. I was opposite the Ladies' Land League. It is worth your while strolling down to look at the exterior decorations of the office; it is really very pretty."

"Thanks. Arabi's flag and that abominable Stars-and-Stripes are quite too much for me. I wonder none of the women thought of spouting off the balcony. You should have made a journey across and have suggested it, and then stood by, a modern Don Quixote, to support these Irish Joans of Arc."[86]

"They might put him on the Executive," laughed another. "Isn't that what they call it? and turn him into a regular Bunthorne. I

---

86. Joan of Arc: (c. 1412–41): the young French woman who became a warrior and subsequently an icon of female heroism, features in newspaper reports about the Ladies' Land League, in their own self-representations (such as Lynch's writing) and later in suffragette discourses of the early twentieth century too.

wonder which of the Joans would bloom into Bunthorne's bride?"

"If I remember rightly," answered Denzil, in his persistent good humour, "Bunthorne didn't succeed in getting a bride at all."

"Ah, you're right. But seriously, Dal, that was a pretty youngster you and Brecknock had on the Adversary a couple of weeks ago. By Jove, I thought I should have died laughing at the sheer audacity of the little minx when she played the "Wearing of the Green" on board ship right in the midst of the Saxons.[87] I thought she was going to sing it, and I was quite ready to help her. I admired her pluck."

Denzil was glad then that Morna had never come to the At Homes on the Adversary; had they began to talk of her in this way—perfectly harmless, but none the less irritating to a properly highfalutin lover—he felt nothing on earth could possibly have restrained him from striking out blindly in furious rage. Not relishing any more of this genial and unattractive conversation he walked out into the Green, and leant on the little bridge where he and Brecknock had seen Marjory standing near the water-edge as they were crossing it. He remembered the pleasure it gave him then because of his wild desire to know something more of Morna. That was six months ago, and where had the desired knowledge left him? To-day Morna was not much nearer to him? He had seen her twice since their last interview and had sorrowfully learnt that that one, brief and painful as it was with all its vague unsatisfactoriness, its intangible bitterness, was the last of the intimate friendship that had made the life of those six months perfect enough for a dream, sweet and pure enough to carry him on into a future however unlike it, however dreary or undesirable, and feel it was worth living from the

---

87. 'Wearing of the Green': 'Irish nationalist song, dating from the end of the 18th century; green had been recognized as the national colour of Ireland since the 17th century, and was adopted particularly by the United Irishmen at the time of the insurrection of 1798'. Knowles, E. (2005). Wearing of the Green. In *The Oxford Dictionary of Phrase and Fable:* Oxford University Press. https://www.oxfordreference.com/view/10.1093/acref/9780198609810.001.0001/acref-9780198609810-e-7633.

lustrous radiance of that time. It had ended as it had begun, perfect, untroubled, stainless. There had been no differences, no harsh words, no silly misunderstandings to blot it, nothing to remember with pain, or that sudden flush of scarlet that the cheek catches from the shame which the memory of a hasty or hard word deepens.

If her beauty and goodness had filled him with a subtle, selfish yearning to keep such harmonious graciousness for "the little while longer" of his whole life, he at least could relinquish the sweet hope, not without passionate regret, but surely without a trace of bitter feeling, without a feeling of jealousy, for the rival she had chosen. Through the wavering lights of his imagination, with on the one side the grand, serene eyes of Morna helping him through the days, and on the other the poor, lifeless shadow of what those days would be without them, he almost thought he could promise to be that man's best friend for the sake of being sometimes near Morna. But did the objection and consequent coldness come from Morna or from Hamilton? When he spoke to her now what was it that seemed to subtly thrust her aloof from him, where her form and face alone seemed pencilled out in cold remoteness, like a statue pencilled in the air, with lips telling no tale, with eyes resolutely veiling the soul beneath? What was it in her that gave him that curious, despairing feeling of one on shore gazing out from aching, grief-weighted eyelids in mute forlornness and helplessness at some beloved form disappearing forever? Could the influence of Hamilton's jealousy be so strong upon her as to make her thus suddenly irresponsive to that depth of humanity within her, so personal and yet so impersonal, and make her act towards him now with such singular capriciousness? Well, be it so. On next Saturday the Adversary would move to Belfast, and he would not return to Dublin afterwards; he would apply for active service, and whenever he remembered his station at Roiville he would have much to be thankful—deeply thankful for. At some future date he would return and visit all the familiar haunts connected with his love for that sweet woman; it would have much, no doubt, of the impassional mournfulness with which one visits the grave of some beloved dead "after long years of grief and pain,"[88] but there would be a soothing tenderness in it, too. And then, perhaps, Morna and Herbert would receive him as the ghost of a friend and forget the disappointed lover, and he would gaze with strange and curious eyes on Morna's children. Who had not dreamed these sort of dreams sometime, and taken a wild delight in probing a wound with pictures furthest calculated from curing it?

He turned at last from these retrospective and future visions, and walked hurriedly towards Hamilton's lodgings.

Herbert Mercer Hamilton was engaged on his historical work when Denzil was ushered into his studio—a charming den, lined with books and valuable engravings. He rose, pen in hand and face gloomily set, at the sight of his rival.

"Can I be of any service to you, sir?" he asked, coldly.

"I have not come to speak of myself, Mr. Hamilton," said Denzil, rushing at once to the point of his visit, "but of Miss Maurice."

"What the devil, sir, have you to say to me of Miss Maurice? I should have thought you were gentleman enough to recognise the extraordinary indelicacy of speaking to me on such a matter," sneered Hamilton.

All this was certainly in keeping with Denzil's pre-conception of Hamilton as an accepted and infuriated lover. He kept his temper admirably, and answered with that grave, steady look which was the wonder and envy of Brecknock.

"I did not see, Mr. Hamilton, that there was anything specially indelicate in my coming to speak to you of my impressions on Miss Maurice's state of health. I don't think there is anything in the object of my visit to you—intrusion, I'm greatly afraid, from your attitude to me, you regard it—unbefitting the conduct of a gentleman."

---

88. 'Oh That 'Twere Possible' from *Maud* (1855), Alfred, Lord Tennyson (1809–1892).

"I know nothing of your nonsensical talk about gentlemen," fiercely interrupted Hamilton.

"Pardon me, Mr. Hamilton," said Denzil, with his courtier-like courtesy, "if you remember, it was you yourself who referred to the question of a gentleman's duties first. I should never have thought of introducing the topic otherwise."

"For heaven's sake, let us have an end to this drawing-room preluding. I'm a man, sir, and you're another; then, in the name of all that's rational, be straightforward, if you can, and speak out the object of your visit—you are right, sir, I call it an unwarrantable intrusion, and I would be glad to have it explained, and gladder still to have done with it," said Hamilton in that low, intense voice which with him was the extremest verge of passion. Each regarded the other as his successful rival, and each marvelled greatly at the attitude of the other. For an accepted lover, Hamilton found Denzil decidedly melancholy; suggestive of mawkish resignation—a suggestion not at all complimentary to the woman who had chosen him, and for which he would dearly have loved to kick him downstairs. On the other hand, Denzil found Hamilton rather more fiercely anticipative of rivalry, rather more explosively jealous, than is the ordinary conception of a fortunate lover. It made him sad to have to think of the madonna serenity of Morna's life worried and humanised in an unnoble way by the Othello-like[89] infirmity of this eccentric.

"I wanted to ask you to counsel Miss Maurice to take rest and change, both of which she badly needs. Her sister even assures me that she is in ill-health."

Denzil's look and voice were such as to place his earnestness beyond a doubt even in the suspicious mind of Hamilton.

"Why?" returned Denzil, staring a little, "because you surely are most interested in the matter. I don't say you are, mind; but unless I am greatly mistaken you ought to be."

---

89. Othello: Shakespeare's eponymous hero whose fatal flaw is jealousy.

"I fail to see the 'ought to be,'" sneered Hamilton, with his passionate dark look. "But even granting the 'is'—mind, I acknowledge even to you the deep interest I take in everything concerning that lady, and which, I beg to tell you, sir, it will always be my most sacred privilege to take—do you still persist in that seaworthy density of intelligence which blinds you to the strange indelicacy of a conversation of this nature between you and me?"

"Good heavens! did anyone ever hear of such blind unreasoning jealousy," cried Denzil, shaken at last out of his exquisite courtesy into real anger. "What has the fact of our both loving the one woman to do with it when she has already chosen between us? As long as I am willing to forget your position towards her, and, consequently, towards me, why should you choose thus to harp on it in that absurd way? Really, Mr. Hamilton, the indelicacy is entirely yours. If I wanted to act the aggrieved party I would perhaps be a little within my right, but I came here to-day to speak to you on this matter, in case you had not been so struck with Miss Maurice's condition as I, and to part friends with you."

They were both standing now, and the angry light in Denzil's fine, blue eyes had died away to contemptuous coldness as he thrust one hand into the breast of his outer coat and lifted up his hat and gloves with the other. Hamilton was glaring at him like a caged lion, and, before answering him, began to pace up and down in passionate restless rage. Why the devil could he not strike the fellow as he stood there, with his handsome, high-bred face so naturally attractive to a woman's fastidious eye? How could he expect Morna to be above the attraction of those strong and delicate features, that picturesque abundance of fair hair relieving the pale bronze face and clear, sea-blue eyes with that nameless, mythical grace of centuries running through his movements, his voice, and manners? Until now, Hamilton had been too busy and calm to know much about the strong passion of hate, but if hate were enough to blast the life, the being, and happiness of another, Denzil Dalrymple was assuredly a doomed man. His strong, honest nature could stand this sort of acting and cold repression no longer. He burst out suddenly, pausing before Denzil:

"What do you mean, sir? Have you come here to insult me? To prate about indelicacy and jealousy and your willingness to forget that I had had the coolness to love the woman you have condescended to set your beggarly, half-blooded heart on? Let me tell you, sir, that I regard your offer of friendship as the shallow outcome of insolent puppyism. Your friendship, forsooth! When you have blasted my life and happiness and caused years of devotion to be flung back on me unresponded to, unthought of! You with your affected humbug, your trash about metaphysics and transcendentalism, your young ladyish raptures over infernal stuff like 'Daniel Deronda,' your faith and unfaith, and your soulful appeals against agnosticism, the regular hackneyed stock-in-trade sentimentalism; your confounded music, and that 'you-and-I' mannerism which is so sickening and repulsive to the healthy masculine mind, but which women— God help them—even the best of them, even Morna, cannot help taking an ineffable delight in. There, because you are handsome and distinguished-looking, with a list of ancestors and the Lord knows what else besides, because you can lisp out your sweet aspirations and fluttering fears of the world to come, I'm thrown over after years of hope and devotion; thrown over for your boyish nonsense. Oh, there is nothing in me, of course. I don't play the violin till women's eyes fill with tears and strange depths are stirred within them; my brains are not addled with idle speculations, and I don't look at a woman with my whole soul gathered into my eyes till any other rational man present would give the world to strike the light out of my eyes. Those, sir, are a list of your womanish accomplishments, and God help my beautiful, holy Morna when she comes to the end of them, and finds for what she has so readily sacrificed a strong man's strong heart and boundless devotion. I never knew a fellow of your manners and exterior attractions to be true yet to the one woman who loves you. Because you are handsome and finished in fascination you can't content yourself at one shrine. You must go about fluttering like an insipid, flirting butterfly, sipping the dew-mists of one woman's eyes, inhaling the scent of another woman's hair, breathing out your whole soul on some other lips redder and richer than the last you kissed. But I am not of this make. I have troubled myself with no other woman's lips to examine if they were red or soft. They were not hers, and that was all I cared to know of them. I have looked into no woman's eyes in love but the one, and they are worth all the black and hazel, the brown and blue eyes of the universe. I am no saint, sir; I've scored some follies to my account, which I cannot remember without unspeakable shame and sorrow because of one clear-eyed saint, with calm, mild brows and tender smiles; but I have loved but one woman in the course of a life which has run out thirty-three years, and you cannot swear as much to her."

Up to his reference to his own blasted life and hopes, Denzil had listened to his first furious retort in cold amazement, but as he burst on gathering passion with his speed like a mountain rapid, all Denzil's being was thrilled into immeasurable, incoherent joy. Morna had refused him; here was the solution of Hamilton's furious reception of himself. That was hope in itself. But what was Hamilton conveying to him in that strange reference to a preference for himself? Could that be Morna's secret, and could she have unveiled it to Hamilton? Oh, no; such a want of reticence would have been a blot on his grand ideal of her stainless maidenhood, and wild with passion and delight, as it would have made him, the happiness would have been too dearly bought at the priceless worth of that white rectitude. It must be simply the distorted outcome of Hamilton's enraged imagination. He tried to veil the gladness of his gaze, and spoke very gently:—

"Excuse me, Mr. Hamilton, you will cease to look on me so blackly, I am sure, when I explain to you that we have both been labouring under serious misapprehension. I have been regarding you as Miss Maurice's accepted husband. I am in the precise position of yourself, in spite of your unjust accusations; no other woman ever has been or ever can be to me what she has been to me in the past six months, and yet I did not hate you, because I thought your assured position towards her made all hope to me impossible; I was just enough to you to recognise your superior gifts and merits, especially that of a longer devotion—I will not say a deeper. I could yet be friendly to you, because I could look back on the sweetest past a man could aspire to—friendship, intimacy with the best and purest woman he had known. But because of this—because of the hope I had once cherished, it had been my intention, when the time of your marriage neared, to apply for active service. I can understand too well the sorrow you feel, if, as you say, you are no nearer to her than myself; as for your other inference I disregard it, because she has given me no reason to suppose it true, and she can scarcely have given you any."

"How dare you say such a thing to me?" cried Hamilton, beside himself. "Now, look here, sir. I've had quite enough of you and your maudlin sentiment, so you had better leave me before I'm tempted to throw you downstairs. I love this girl still, better than life, and will in spite of you, even if she has you."

Denzil troubled himself with no further friendly overtures, but left, a little drunk with joy.

CHAPTER XXIII

A CURIOUS ENDING OF COURTSHIP.

The next day was the day of the torpedo practising, and Denzil accompanied the Maurices and Brecknock home from Roiville, with the hope of seeing Morna. He saw something had occurred between Marjory and young Harston, and though the nature of the difference he could not guess, he was beginning to believe it not improbable that his friend was on a fair way to bloom into society, at no impossible date, as a converted Benedict, with the most witching and maddening little Beatrice conceivable.[90] Of course, it was difficult to know in how far Marjory might be serious and how much of it might be only flirting on her part, which he was inclined to suspect. She had never looked more charming than on the Adversary that morning. She wore something soft and brilliant in colour in the shape of a summer dress—several shades of blue blended into one—with black lace gather thickly around her neck, in startling contrast with its purity of colour and outline in a strange-looking, black velvet cap rested on the hair that had been washed the day before, and was consequently most unmanageable and flossy, waving and curling and fluttering in every impossible way, and in every hue between the brightest gold and the softest fairest silver. It would have delighted Denzil if Harston could just have seen her and heard her laugh. It would not have soothed that little cad's vanity to know his absence could not dim her radiance.

As for Brecknock, all his scruples on the question of birth, politics, religion had been finally overcome, and he was now lazily afloat on a sea of most perfect satisfaction, where he found nothing more reasonable than the condition of loverhood, nobody so lovely and merry as Marjory, and nothing more natural than his desire to secure her for himself. She would be sure not to worry a fellow with any whims but the most delightful and unanalytical, such as an innocent preference for candied sweets and tarts—he rather liked sweets and tarts himself—who would feed on arrowroot (a favourite form of nutriment with him), and look sparkling on the evanescent foam of champagne, and whose wildness would bring into marriage striking originality enough to make the condition amiable. He would not, perhaps, relish her indulging in any freak

---

90. Benedict and Beatrice: leading characters in Shakespeare's *Much Ado about Nothing* (1600).

too *outré* in the presence of others, but an occasional cigarette, now, when they would be by themselves, by Jove! that would be quite fetching. And then to watch her giving orders and throwing over her mistakes a bewildering fascination which would insure them against the tame insipidity of correctness or perfection! He would enjoy the mistakes tremendously, provided they did not quite extend to the regulation of dinner. Well no, his fine good nature could not really be expected to embrace delightedly the possibilities of a bad dinner. Of course, Marjory would be too much a lady not to recognise the importance of this department and be careful not to put his temper to the test of such a severe ordeal. He had developed the fatal trick of smiling much when alone and shaking his head in keen enjoyment whenever a sudden attitude, or look, or gesture of Marjory's started before him, and he was persuaded that a certain way she had of lifting her eyelid, so that the long, curled lashes seemed to touch the brown above, and looking at your over her shoulder in coquettish gravity, was the very finest thing in the world.

He sent her boxes of sweets, flowers, fruit, and gloves as often as he could decorously contribute to such little feminine comforts, and, for a slow, indolent fellow like him, proved himself amazingly cultured in his condition as aspiring lover. Marjory accepted all his attentions and presents, as though they were the most natural thing in life. Perhaps she thought at first that it would be easy to overcome her love for Frank and settle down to unregretful matrimony with this clumsy, good-natured Romeo; but the last quarrel with Frank showed her the horrible tenacity of her love, and, though determined not to give in to her sorrows, but to battle with it unceasingly until she should have conquered it—that is, if Frank were not to return to her— she felt her widowhood strong upon her. Alone, the immense passion of regret would bear down upon her resistance, swamping all her new-learnt lessons of fortitude and pride, her girl's light philosophy in that cry:—

"O that 'twere possible
After long grief and pain
To find the arms of my true love
Round me once again."[91]

It was a mania with her to moan the lines to herself between little, gasping, shuddering sobs, and feel that life now could yield her no other sorrow since the light of love had gone out of it. Morna watched the first overmastering swell of grief in silence, content to bring into it the soothing influence of tenderest sisterhood with no idle consolation. She knew enough of life and grief to know how much must spend itself into thorough exhaustion before comfort can enter. She hoped eventually that she would grow out of it all and marry Brecknock, yet she sometimes dreaded that the effect on the girl would be lasting.

She hated to think of Hamilton—perhaps, too, baffling with the sorrow of regret—and fretted and worried herself about her friend and sister in a woman's persistent Quixotism.[92] Few of them escape the nature or, as Mrs. Barrett Browning calls it, their "woman's trade to suffer torment for another's ease."[93]

She did not wait for the return of her uncle and Marjory from Roiville, as one of her colleagues was ill and she had made arrangements to remain with her all night. In vain poor Denzil signed to Brecknock to wait, and at last went away bitterly disappointed. The next day was Friday, and the Adversary was to leave Roiville early on Saturday morning.

Brecknock on leaving Leeson-street had managed to slip a note into Marjory's hand asking for a definite answer to the proposal she must have known he was waiting to make her for sometime past. He would call about noon next day and learn his fate which

---

91. 'Oh That 'Twere Possible' from *Maud* (1855). See note 88.
92. Quixotism: probably a reference to Tabitha Gilman Tenney's *Female Quixotism* (1801), a novel tracing a series of misadventures for the heroine, Dorcasina Sheldon, in pursuit of romantic love.
93. Quotation from Elizabeth Barrett Browning's *Aurora Leigh* (1856).

he hoped would be in accordance with his desire. The declaration was manly and frank, and brief as should be the ideal declaration of a sailor, and Marjory felt touched beyond the inevitable thrill of girlish vanity and pleasure. But immediately afterwards her strong love for Frank rushed in upon her, dissolving the trembling satisfaction into passionate tears, and she felt how impossible it would be to hope for cure in another affection; how repugnant to her was the thought of love unconnected with Frank. Marjory was a very natural girl—frivolous, impressionable, short-tempered, and changeable. I have no intention of presenting her to my readers as an ideal of fidelity or deep passion; she would have been glad enough to have married Brecknock, and, to put it in her own original vernacular, "dash Harston in the face," but the feat was morally and physically beyond her. She sorrowed for her lost love with a sorrow beyond her; saw him everywhere, felt him everywhere, missed him everywhere. She knew that if she married any other man she would grow to hate him fiercely, simply because he was not Frank. She knew she could never be reconciled to go through the days without looking forward to meeting him somewhere at the end of them. The misery of expectation and hope deferred was even better than the utter, hopeless, blank wretchedness that looks forward to nothing but its own shadowy self. If she married Brecknock or any other, would there ever come a to-morrow that would not find her like yesterday peering through streets and gathered assemblies with wondering, yearning eyes for the only face she desired to see, listening eagerly for the one voice that thrilled her with the sweet, inward music of gladness? If it could be otherwise; if she could hope to forget him and cease to hunger for his smile and caress, she would have married Brecknock—firstly, because she really liked him and his position, that was so much beyond her aspirations, even though she knew he was somewhat partial to champagne and brandy; but that was a common failing with men, and Frank had something of the weakness, too, she believed.

When Brecknock arrived at Leeson-street he was told that Marjory had a bad headache and given a letter. This did not look like a favourable response to his overture certainly, and his faculties were a little numbed in apprehension as he opened the letter:

"Dear Mr. Brecknock—Your letter, conveying a proposal which I feel a very great honour, indeed, makes me angry with myself in the knowledge that I have been unfair to you. I will be candid and acknowledge to you that I knew you wished me to believe that you cared for me, and yet I never showed you that it would be impossible for me to marry you. I am very, very sorry, though I have not the right to ask you to believe me when I say so. Perhaps when I tell you that I don't feel very strong lately, and that I am unhappy, you will try not to feel quite harshly towards me, because I like you ever so much, and would gladly accept your kind proposal if I could. May I call myself

"Your sincere friend,

"Marjory?"

This poor pathetic little letter vanquished all Arthur's sense of being alighted or unfairly used. The hint in it of unhappiness and struggle stirred old fibres of manliness and chivalry within him, and made him wish the girl had a mother, until he remembered Morna. He pictured her crying upstairs, perhaps, and he would have liked to have gone and comforted her in a soothing, brotherly way, and protested he was so fond of her as was possible without any further matrimonial intentions. He kissed the note and put it into his pocket, feeling better and kinder because it was there, and scrawled on a pocket-sheet:

"Don't think I could be angry with you, Marjory. You'll always be the best and dearest little girl in the world to me. Good-by.

"A. B."

(To be Continued—Commenced in No. 949.)

CHAPTER XXIV

A CONVERSATION ON BOARD SHIP.

Denzil had made two ineffectual efforts to see Morna on Friday, and left Roiville after a sleepless night, harassed and pained in the conviction that she had been purposely avoiding him. Since Hamilton's passionate outburst he had had no opportunity of declaring his own condition and hope to her, and now there were only two alternatives before him: a two month's silence—achingly apprehensive to contemplate—or a written proposal. That was specially repugnant to him. He wanted, in confessing his love, to have the dear delight or pain of watching its effect on her face. If she refused him, there would be something more soothing in the delicate music of her voice than in a refusal coldly traced on paper. The delay held many consequences nicely balanced, it is true, but it is never quite unendurable while Hope holds its light aloft and lends its wonderful mystical hues to the gloom of dread.

He stood watching the country sweeping round the coast with that sense of vague forlornness which the consciousness of being carried away by impersonal force from something familiar and unspeakably dear leaves. Some ladies and acquaintances were gathered on the pier and at the back of the lighthouse waving farewells to their friends on the vessel—a few naval enthusiasts unacquainted with anyone on board waving handkerchiefs with as much energy as though the captain was their first-cousin and every lieutenant a brother or lover. But his glance was eagerly directed towards Dublin.

Brecknock recognised Evelyn Handcock in a conspicuous

position, and looked through his field glass with the idea that Marjory might have slept in Roiville that night and have come down to wave them a kind good-by. The disappointment when he found she was not there was deeper than he imagined it could be, and he lit a cigar, seeking solace in furious puffs.

"I guess, Den, you and I won't be seen in that queer place in Sackville-street again," he said, gloomily, as he approached Denzil.

"I suppose not," rejoined Denzil, shortly.

"Won't you smoke? Ah, well, would you believe it, Denny, it was the happiest and most innocent time of my life. I suppose it would be idiotic and useless to wish it back again, but I'll never forget those two girls, and whenever I want to think of anyone good enough to make a fellow believe in heaven, I'll think of Miss Maurice, but the little one—she is all that is dearest and sweetest in this world. By Jove, Den, I had no idea I could be so awfully in love before," he said, shaking his head mournfully.

"Why didn't you ask her then?" cried Denzil, impatiently. He was irritated to find his friend in the same predicament as himself.

"I did ask her, but I'm afraid that fellow we met there is in my way, Den, I want your opinion on something. She wrote me this letter, and it's been puzzling me ever since. I'm beginning to fancy that fellow isn't a gentleman; it looks uncommonly like as if he is acting shabbily."

He handed Denzil Marjory's letter with that unconscious reluctance we feel in parting, however momently, with anything we cherish. Denzil took the letter and read it slowly under the eager, questioning gaze of his friend.

"There is no doubt about his shabbiness, Arthur," he said, returning it to him. "He's a cad, and I suspected it would come to this all along. She is a very sweet child, far too good for him, and, if you really cared for her, I don't think, in your place, that I'd let this thing stand in my way—I mean I wouldn't give up hope.

She'll be naturally unhappy about it for some time; but girls, at least some girls, get over these unfortunate love affairs. Of course, I know there is a certain prejudice among us Turks of men against succession in a woman's heart; but, with a fairy like Marjory I don't think it could hold good. She'll go on falling in love until she is married, I suspect, when she'll settle down to the neatest little slip of matronhood imaginable."

"You think she'll get over it?" asked Arthur, with his slow, questioning look.

"I sincerely hope so at any rate."

"Do you know, Denny, I'd give anything to have that fellow here and quietly chuck him overboard, or to have the chance of putting a bullet through him."

"I daresay you would; yet I doubt if he would be worth the trouble or the consequences."

"Well, he must be a shabby, low-bred hound. I'm a bad, worthless sort of fellow, but I wouldn't like Marjory or anybody to think I could be shabby," he said, in pathetic gravity.

Denzil took his hand and shook it warmly by way of response.

Arthur turned away abruptly to hide a decided moisture that the conversation had brought into his eyes, and when he spoke his voice was a little unsteady:—

"I thought you were fixed pretty much in the same way about the other one, Den."

Denzil did not answer at once, but turned his clear, bronze face slowly landward, hunting along the coast for the nearest point of Dublin: he had been used to those confidences from his friend without feeling an inclination to respond to them by similar outbursts, but now that his heart was stirred by such unique apprehension and hopelessness, it drifted in upon him that even Brecknock's dull intelligence when turned upon his case might clear away the shadows.

With one of those precipitate dashes with which the naturally reticent rush into unreserve, he burst out, wheeling suddenly round:—

"Look here, Brecknock, I will tell you all. I am in love with her, wholly, eternally, sacredly. And yet I am leaving her in doubt of the earnestness of my passion, or rather in ignorance of its existence. Can you explain it? I can't. You, at least, were a man. You tempted your fate courageously; but I was a coward. I stood back because I dreaded to hear that Hamilton had been before me. Nothing can excuse it, I know, to have acted right for her and right for me, I should have spoken. What can she think of me now? What does any woman, Brecknock, think of a man who hangs on her words, looks, and wishes as I hung on hers and leaves her then silently, but that he is a most infamous trifler. I don't think so much about her feelings, because I'm afraid she is independent of that part of woman's destiny, but I couldn't bear her to think me a scoundrel, or not a gentleman. I couldn't bear her not to believe I am heart and soul in earnest." He drew a long breath. "That she should think me anything less than her lover, no matter for how short a time, maddens me, and what can I do now but wait in sickening dread of what may be in her mind of me and of what may occur? But she must know how it is with me, she must. Don't women always know?" he asked," in passionate urgence, more meekly than his custom.

The question was too important for a prompt answer. Brecknock thought awhile, then said, shaking his head gravely:—

"You used to know more about women's minds than I, Den, at least you had a lot of theories on hand. But, as far as I can guess, she must know; you made yourself noticeably her lover, and I don't see how she could think anything else. But, about your silence, that's another affair. It looks a little shabby, you know. A fellow should have something to say for himself after six months as you've had. But, say, Den, what's to prevent your writing?" he ended, with a sudden brilliant thought.

Denzil started backward with a gesture of repugnance and vexation.

"If I were a woman I wouldn't like to receive written proposals. They are cold and formal. Then, she mightn't have me, and I couldn't bear to get a written refusal. No, I'd prefer to judge my chances from her face!"

"But, why didn't you ask her?" said Brecknock, returning to the question, in persistent wonder.

"That's just it, why didn't I? To tell you the truth, Brecknock, she has been avoiding me lately, and I think Hamilton is the cause of it. She refused him, and I fancy he got jealous, and attached her about me. It was a damnable liberty on his part, and"—

"It put a nail in your coffin, you think," interrupted Brecknock, seriously. "Yes, that sort of thing would make a girl fight shy of a fellow. But, if you say she's refused Hamilton—a right good sort of chap he was, I can tell you—then I don't see where's your difficulty. There's no other fellow goes there but that newspaper fellow, and it's after Marjory he is. Did you hear what he said to me one day: 'Now, listen to me, Mr. Brecknock, I don't want you to be making a fool of yourself, hankering after Miss Marjory Maurice. That young woman's been a-growing up for me as another young woman once grew up for Mr. Dick Swiveller, if you ever heard of that remarkable person.'"[94]

Brecknock laughed and lit another cigarette but Denzil's echo of his laugh was very melancholy.

"I have no male rival I know, but I may have a worse or rather a more difficult rival to manage," he said musingly.

"Hang it, man, what do you mean?"

"She is very religious," he said questioningly.

"Oh, is that what you mean? But she has too much sense to lock herself up in a nunnery."

---

94. Mr Dick Swiveller: a devious character who becomes a force for good in Charles Dickens' *Old Curiosity Shop*.

Denzil turned and walked about, then he halted abruptly, and put his hand on Brecknock's arm.

"I don't know what I think or what I fear, except this, that if Miss Maurice refuses me I will be a perfectly wretched man, and that I will never love any woman as I love her. As for how I'm to get through the next two months—the question is beyond me; I regard the horror of it in sheer desperation," he groaned.

"Oh, it'll not be as bad as that, old fellow," said Brecknock, soothingly. "I rather guess when you get into the swing of it you'll pull along like any of us. If she thinks a little badly of you now, she'll think all the better of you by and by when she knows how you've felt about it."

"Yes, but it is horrible all the same," said Denzil, with a wan smile, and speaking rather huskily.

"I tell you what it is, Den, I feel bad enough myself when I think of that little girl in trouble, and I not able to take care of her," said his friend after a long pause, and breaking into a short rueful laugh. "It's rather different then the last time we shoved out together."

CHAPTER XXV

MARJORY'S TRIAL

Brecknock was right, when he pictured Marjory's clear, star-like eyes, blurred with tear-mists, her little scarlet mouth shaken with trembling sobs, as he left the house. His manly straightforward declaration and his rough unorthodox assertion, in reply to her missive, thrilled her with wild regret, to find herself so hopelessly, helplessly bound to that other, who made her chain so bitter—so full of pain—so unendurable from doubt. What was it in women that made them cling in stupid fidelity to the wrong man? It sounds anomalous; but, if Harston had caused her less trouble—less heartache and tears—she would, probably, have found it an easier after to thrust away his memory and the false responsibilities of a fidelity which ought to have been irksome, and which certainly had no *raison d'éetre*. I am obliged to paint my little heroine, with whom I am as much in love as ever was Trollope[95] with his favourite heroines—as sorrowing and suffering for a worthless, effete specimen of manhood, simply because she suffered and sorrowed; but I would infinitely prefer to picture her philosophically indifferent and sensibly engaged to that harmless fellow on sea. But girls are rarely philosophers, especially if they have once had the misfortune to fall in love; then they become absolute idiots, though men, in order possibly to look picturesque and complaisant, somewhat falsely assume that privilege. So Marjory was, of course, idiotic, but she showed much bravery. She never wrote a line to Frank though her heart was sore within her and the temptation terribly great. In public her spirits never flagged, her wit was nothing less unsociable and startling. From her appearance and manner no one could guess that the small heart within her was breaking, and that the greater part of her nights was spent in tears, or in tearless, moaning sobs much more exhaustive.

Frank wrote at the end of a fortnight. The letter was not much, a piece of intimate curt impertinence, but it was enough to open afresh those appalling shivers of passion and regret. She read it and placed it with other love-missives in days when her lover could write tenderly or passionately. The letter remained there unanswered, and those who know anything of love will understand the immense self-restraint this meant, the greater when we remember Marjory's unpretentious girlhood, her unrestrained, impulsive nature, as little given to thought, or introspective analysis, or meditations on self-respect as a forest bird; who merely lived and laughed because it was pleasant, and loved because she loved, and the somebody was—Frank! At the time Morna readily applauded her silence

---

95. Trollope: Anthony Trollope (1815–1882), popular mid-Victorian novelist.

but not long afterwards she bitterly regretted the proud impulse that had urged her to express her approval. That was when in the retraction of remorse, in the wild, helpless, floundering waves of regret, she came to think her wisdom most unwise, her guidance but a blunder.

A few papers and magazines followed the unanswered letter at long intervals, none of which were opened, but resolutely hidden away with all her love-memorials. She visited the Exhibition frequently, attended parties and concerts, laughed and chatted most brilliantly, and wished herself at rest in Glasnevin all the time.[96] Of course it was noticed that she was a thought thinner, but only a thought, and who minds that in sensitive girlhood?

Morna fancied her shoulders something shrunken, her throat slenderer, and her hands paler. She was not exactly alarmed but proposed a visit to Hastings or Wales.

Marjory acquiesced delightedly. This was in the middle of October. Next day Morna was asked if she had heard the report of Harston's engagement to an heiress down in Wicklow. She scarcely credited the report, but pondered on the advisability of acquainting Marjory with it. Her doubts were yet unsolved when she found her sister, with eyes of dumb pain looking out of her poor pathetic white little face, and reaching a letter towards her with a helpless gesture. The letter was from a friend referring to the report. Morna took the fragile child into her arms, and wept over her. What was there to say? Speak harshly of him? No good. Speaking soothingly of the time of indifference to come? Scarcely better. Morna had not even the heart to refer to the idleness of the report, but Marjory did after a pause of mute grief. Morna was silent, it seemed such pathetic tragic nonsense, her protest in her belief in her lover's truth and honour. Who could be cruel enough to awaken her to the rudeness, the bleak nakedness of reality? Morna listened to her

---

96. Glasnevin: Glasnevin Cemetery in Dublin dating from 1832. Lynch's stepfather, James Cantwell, who died in 1873, was buried there as well as several siblings and half siblings who predeceased Lynch.

passionate outburst silently, sadly, but made no effort to shake the child's conviction. The blow came soon enough, and when it came it was a terrible, a cruelly terrible hour. Morna glanced through the paper over her solitary breakfast, and her breath stopped suddenly and then came in short, scared gasps as she read in a paragraph devoted to county fashionable intelligence the marriage of Francis Harston and Louisa Trediger, of Wicklow, &c. She read it over twice before she realised the horror of the announcement, and then her head fell upon her arms, gathered over the paper, with a cry of mighty anguish. She thought of her child, her one strong love, upstairs, sleeping and unconscious, perhaps dreaming of this wretched scoundrel; she thought of her white face and big, clear, blue eyes, her laugh as spontaneous as a thrush's song, her wild, free movements, all that indescribable, unconscious poetry of girlhood not yet free of the scent of childhood; of her loveliness, her brightness, her inexhaustible wit and quaintness, and wished that she herself had died rather than this tragedy had happened. She moaned and sobbed and writhed in the appalling helplessness of her agony. What could she do to lessen the outrage? What could she do to soothe the child's wild anguish? For a moment, fixed in the utter hopelessness of the task before her, she almost wished that those sweet, blue eyes upstairs might never open again.

She went into Marjory's room very softly. The girl had just awakened, and was sitting up. Morna went over to her and put her arms around her in appealing gentleness. Marjory stared at her sad face and wet eyelids in apprehensive alarm.

"You have heard something about Frank?" she gasped in quick, short breaths.

"Yes, darling. Will you try to be strong and brave, and remember that no matter what you may have to suffer I will always love you better than all the world?" said Morna.

"You've heard that the report's true?—that he is married—or dead?" insisted Marjory.

"Not dead, darling."

The voice was low, but the eyes thrillingly sad and tender. Marjory gazed on her in fascinated terror, and demanded imperiously:

"Show me the proof."

"Here is the paper. Be brave, my own, my own little sister," urged Morna, vaguely.

She read the announcement through unflinchingly, and when she laid down the paper her face was white and rigid, her eyes dulled to the utmost deadness compatible with life.

"It is all over now, but what matter?" she whispered, and her whole form shivered with cold.

"Lie down, dearest, and let me bring you up some tea, do," entreated Morna, wishing she would cry out or rave instead of shivering there with that terrible corpse-like look.

"No; leave me, Morna—only for a little while."

She locked the door after her sister, and sat shuddering and tearless on the edge of the bed, like one in a cold nightmare. She took up the paper and read the fatal paragraph again, and then she burst into a wild, shrill laugh that startled even herself, and set her listening for its echo or repetition.

"I suppose I must be going mad," she said, in a low, vague way, holding her head between her hands. Her hands were very cold, and she crept into bed only conscious of an anxiety for physical warmth. But she grew colder, her teeth chattered horribly, and she found herself laughing again. This terrified her, and in a thrill of fright at her own strange society, she hurried to unlock the door when she heard Morna outside.

CHAPTER XXVI

A LOVE SCENE.

Marjory lay in the maze of a short cerebral attack, but she gallantly struggled through it, and at the end of the week, had regained her reason by sheer force of her own indomitable will, and was able to come downstairs, where she took up her invalid position between the sofa and the arm-chair, with Morna as her watchful and tender nurse. Her uncle would sit staring at her helplessly, conscious of his impotence to stamp on that "infernal blackguard," and his equal impotence to bring back the light of life and laughter to that poor little white-face he so thoroughly loved. These long, silent stares generally ended in a rude pathetic effort to make her laugh, somewhat resembling the gambols of a huge mastiff trying to gain the sympathy of a child or a smaller dog in pain. All this great wealth of love was very sweet and soothing to Marjory. She basked in it, revelled in it, and liked to feign little wants for the mere value of the passionate alacrity with which these two great-hearted people rushed to anticipate them. And outside everybody was amazingly kind. All her late colleagues wrote and called constantly, fruit and other such tributes of health in friendship poured in gladdeningly. Even Evy Handcock offered to stay and help Morna to nurse her. There was so much breathless pathos in her story, a position that would be strong in a novel, that every one of these gentle hearts trembled in impersonal grief. Indeed, if genuine hatred and contempt could help to mar any man's honeymoon, Harston's ought to have been one of memorial bitterness. Marjory was converted into a heroine of romance, and his name was enough to call forth a torrent of invectives. Power called and told her he was "damned glad she was out of the whole affair and that he'd shoot that fellow only he was too grateful to him, as his blackguardism gave her a chance to turn back on himself."

This was charming and original wooing, and Marjory would not have been herself if it had not extracted a ripple of her old laughter. Like nearly everybody who called, he sat there gazing on her in helpless sympathy and affection. Hamilton came constantly. He said little to Morna, but satisfied Morna by his great devotion to Marjory. He would carry her into the garden when the sun shone, wrap her shawl gently round her, and read to her if she cared for reading or rummage his brains for the best anecdotes slumbering there. His tenderness and attentions made Marjory plead his suit warmly with Morna. Then one day just as he had left, and Marjory lying back in her chair had relapsed into her terrible grief, with cheeks forlornly wan, and thick blue shadows under her sad eyes, Morna was startled by Denzil's card. She went to him, and he was standing by the window, with eyes strained in wide expectancy towards the door, waiting for the face of those two months' dreams—the pure, palely-lit, spiritual face—and was only conscious of something so different, so intensely sad and white, that he was shocked into silent staring, not unmingled with the overmastering sensation that this evidence of deep grief might be due to his silence.

Neither spoke, but stood gazing mutely, perhaps dreading the first speech. At last Denzil broke out incoherently:

"I don't know that I have any right to explain to you: the existence of the right, I know, depends on your feeling, your attitude towards me, and of that I am in utter ignorance; but I could not bear that you should believe that I went away in August silent because—because I had not anything to say, I had—I had, you must know I had; and yet I left it unsaid because I was afraid. I thought you had accepted another, and did not want to mar your happiness by a futile declaration of feelings which, with your great personal tenderness, could only make you unhappy to know of. And then, when I learnt it was not so, you plainly avoided me, and I could not say anything. I have been so miserable and wretched, fearing you should think meanly of me all this time; for you know a man should speak when he has shown as plainly as I how deeply he loves."

He paused for breath, and stood gazing at her beseechingly. He saw a swift light flash delicately rosily over cheek and brow, striking a deeper brilliance and colour into her clear grey eyes. She moved towards him and rested her hand on his arm in something of a child's way. The mute assurance of her eyes and gesture thrilled him wonderingly. Was it all true? This grand, spiritually cold woman, with her hand upon his arm, and great eyes of yearning happiness fastened upon him in all the candour and simplicity of a mere unquestioning child. He was too much afraid of the nature of her trust to take her in his arms and sob out his own deep joy and wonder. His only answer was to lift the beseeching hand to his lips.

"I will confess it now. Your silence pained me greatly; it made me very lonely."

"Morna, Morna, is this true? I am not dreaming; you are not dreaming; but we are really giving and receiving that brightest, holiest blessing in life—an assurance of mutual love? But, Morna, you have not said that one word yet. Is it love? Tell me," he urged passionately.

She moved away from him and sat down.

"I think it is love, though I never thought to have felt it. Tell me you [sic]. The days have been longer and drearier, because you were away; I have wakened during the night with an aching sense that I have mistook your meaning, and that you left me in silence simply because you did not care for me as I had imagined. I thought of all your actions and words and looks, and felt miserable in the thought that you had not acted well; but then I think I was lonelier for you than anything. I am glad now. Is that love?"

"Why, Morna, my beautiful grey-eyed saint, this is sweet, simple, human love. You child, not to know it," he cried, flinging himself on a low chair at her feet, and sitting there with clasped hands in her lap and happy eyes.

"Morna, I want to ask you a question, not that I really doubt your answer, for I know so intimately what it will be. But I merely wish to reassure myself of the truth of my own conviction. Tell me have you ever thought of love before?"

She looked at him gravely, and reflected a bit, then her face broke into a smile.

"I remember now, but it was a long time ago, and I scarcely knew what I was thinking about. Some girls brought me with them to see the gypsies when I was twelve years of age, and one of the women insisted on telling me my fortune, too. All I remembered of it was that I was to fall in love at fifteen. That made a great impression on me, and when I was fifteen I looked around me curiously. I only know one man, and him I did not know, but he was intimate with papa, and very picturesque-looking. I used to wonder when I would be able to paint such thick-brown curls as his, and such dark blue eyes, with their curious trick of opening widely and seriously. But I was always afraid of him, and would blush horribly if he spoke to me. Once or twice he caught me looking at him very earnestly when I was thinking of what the gypsies said, and I nearly died of shame because I felt sure he read my thought. I was so ashamed that I could never bear to see him again."

It was a very simple and inconsequent confession, but it startled Denzil uncomfortably. It was repugnantly unlike his ideal of her white, unconscious maidenhood, and he felt fiercely furious against those gypsies and the wretched girls who, in taking a mere child with them, had taught her how to spell the word love—well, perhaps, not to spell it, but to ponder on it and pronounce it deep within her own child's heart. That was not the unknowing, clear-eyed, Galatea-like ideal he had been worshipping.[97] He felt he had been stupidly deprived of the grand knowledge that he had stirred the unconscious depths of her soul, into which no man's eyes or image had gazed; that his thought had been the first

---

97. Galatea-like: relating to Ovid and ideals of womanhood. Galatea is the 'name of an ivory statue of a woman carved by the sculptor Pygmalion, who fell in love with his own creation'. Delahunty, Andrew and Sheila Dignen. Galatea" *A Dictionary of Reference and Allusion:* Oxford University Press. *Oxford Reference.* <https://www.oxfordreference.com/view/10.1093/acref/9780199567454.001.0001/acref-9780199567454-e-742>.

to quicken her pulses in sweet wonder; that the word "love" had first leaped into her mind at his confession. And it would have been so but for this silly, trivial child's nonsense. He might have hugged his consciousness in the belief that a nature so formed, so womanly in all things else, was in this region as ignorant, as blindly reliant, as a new-born child, or as an infant just struggling to walk and clinging fearfully to the nurse's hand. But, after all, she was scarcely less a child, with that wonderful unkissed mouth and those clear eyes, love-lit for the first time, because at fifteen she had gazed in furtive wonder and apprehension at a young man, and pondered vaguely on an idle story told her by a gypsy. Had he no tale to tell?

"Have you thought of what this all means?" he asked, at length, possessing himself of her hand. "Of our being together always in the perfect years of marriage stretching on before us goldenly."

"No, no; don't speak of it. I forgot. Marjory is very ill. I cannot marry, I must give my life to her. She is so unhappy."

"But I, Morna, am I not to be thought of as well as Marjory? I am willing to abide by any decision of yours that will not separate us. You can't even now know what love is, or you wouldn't propose anything so monstrous as to leave me out of your life."

"But you don't understand," she tried to explain, but all her womanly assurance and confidence had vanished, and she was very anxious and beseeching in his hands. "How can I think of my own happiness when she is so miserable and ill? Indeed, I wonder I can ever believe in your love after her sad experience."

"Good God! You are not going to class honourable, honest men with a ruffian like that, I hope. And do you really believe it will make Marjory happier in the knowledge that our happiness has been sacrificed to a mere whim."

"It is no whim. Don't make it worse for me," she urged, tearfully. "We must take her away. She is very, very ill."

"And is this to last always, Morna? If she should not live?"

The words were scarcely out of his mouth before he would have given anything to recall them. He wondered when he should forget the look of dumb anguish and reproach she turned on him.

"You are cruel to speak of that. But if she dies I shall leave the world. I could not endure it, even with your love, without her."

"You are trying to punish me now," he cried, bitterly. "I can understand much, but this surpasses me. Do I look grieved, Morna, for heaven knows how I feel? Well, consider me punished and repentant, and retract that horrible threat. I know you are too good for me; you are too good for any man, but I, at least, have the merit of having the priceless gift of your love. Does that mean nothing in my favour? Is your woman's nature so slight and strange that you can throw away this feeling like a mere toy, instead of treasuring it like the immeasurable, eternal blessing it is? But no, this convent life is a fancy you have always had, and you naturally find it strange at once to abandon it, but try to tell yourself now the nature of my sacred right; try to understand that nothing should alter your purpose to take me into your life."

"I have thought of it. If my life were to be cast in the lines of happiness I would gladly, oh! gladly share my joy with you, but my sorrow, no; it will be terrible. I could not blight you with it."

Her reasoning tortured him; he threw himself into a chair and covered his face with his hands.

"It would be less, we two together. Can't you believe that," he broke out in fierce distress.

He felt her hand upon his shoulder and looked up with wet eyes; hers met his in an answering mirage of gaze.

"Nothing but God could bring me comfort in such desolation. We have always been together; what could replace that? I have loved her wholly, alone, when you did not exist for me. If she gets well we may all be happy together, if not, all life will be a sorrow for me."

She glided from him like a vision, and he sat there staring, stupidly, blindly conscious of her absence.

(To be Continued—Commenced in No. 949.)

CHAPTER XXVII

THE LAST.

During the fortnight which followed Denzil was the most assiduous and attentive of Marjory's visitors. The girl was startled by his persistent inquiries about her moods, her feelings and expressions: she looked a little paler than yesterday, but she was not worse? She merely had not slept well, perhaps? In his mind he cursed Harston pretty freely, and seemed to hang on Marjory's looks and words when they referred to her own condition with all the avidity of an ardent lover, instead of one's sister's lover. He daily came supplied with Hamburg grapes and other such luxuries that he could pounce upon; protested strongly against over-exertion, excitement, or depression, watched her, with a breathless despair no less than Morna's, thinning and drooping each day, felt that her laugh was growing fainter and rarer. And then came a day when she could not come downstairs, and everyone knew that it must have gone hard with Marjory when she could be induced by reason or languor to remain in bed an entire day.

Denzil did not see Morna that day, but left Leeson-street with a choking sensation in his throat. Could it be possible, in the event of death, that Morna would persist in her wild refusal of love or comfort?

All her old friends visited Marjory, convinced that the end was not far off. One day she troubled them by a strange insistence, considering her weak and frail condition, on getting up. It was useless to argue with her; she pleaded loneliness, a need of change, insatiable restlessness, and Morna dressed her and lifted her downstairs like the child she was. Denzil and Hamilton had just called and met Power talking to Mr. Maurice in the drawing-room. Some of her intimate friends among the late Ladies' Land League were there awaiting the experiment of moving. Everyone rose as Morna entered with her burden of blue-robed form with its familiar waves of gold rippling round the little white face, the small, vivid mouth and the sweet, pale forget-me-not eyes looking wistfully over the blue shadows beneath. Not one was present unthrilled with great personal delight at the sight and some rushed eagerly to arrange the sofa, the blind, the cushions, and her pillows.

Marjory laughed right out in her old, thoughtless laughter. Involuntarily Morna and Denzil looked at one another and shivered: the gleefulness of it was ghastly, so like an echo from the grave. Morna turned to conceal her tears, and Denzil felt thrust aloof from her because he could not show her that she was not alone in her sorrow. Marjory laughed again at one of Georgina Templeton's frantic efforts to rouse her. This inspired her to break into her old habit of mimicry. She gave a new edition of the much appreciated and pathetic history of the woes of my Lord Silchester, gave a favourite representation of Mark Luke Fitzgerald[98] and other distinguished Irish orators, painted some of them in medieval and others in romantic colours, and all equally and exquisitely ludicrous; told some of her own experiences in her vividest and maddest strain, and was never more excitingly brilliant and witty. She then touched on the past; she, being the principal speaker, of the political movement, told all its best anecdotes and incidents, and ended by protesting anew that the happiest time of her life was the time of the great Convention. She gave the Irish chief

---

98. Mark Luke Fitzgerald: a fictional name but probably a barely concealed allusion to Charles Stewart Parnell or John E. Redmond.

a sincere and impersonal worship, which did not prevent her, nevertheless, from mimicking him best of all.

It was a day of irrational fun and laughter to be remembered by all present.

"Well," she concluded, with a sigh of sheer fatigue, as she lay back among her pillows, "I used to say long ago that if all things else failed me I could always fall back on the position of guide to Glasnevin Cemetery, but now I'm afraid I'm soon going to turn into part of the show myself. Will you come and visit my grave, Mr. Dalrymple, at some future date? I'd propose your examining my skull, only I believe I'm to be deposited in a family-vault—the Irish relic of decency—but sit on the edge of the vault, and say to whoever is with you: 'Alas, poor Marjory! I knew her. She was a girl of infinite mirth.'[99] After all, I don't think anyone will have much worse to say of me."

This speech was listened to in an intense rigid silence. Tears started hotly into the women's eyes, and some few were racking their brains how to reply in proper soothing and denial, when Denzil, shocked and pained beyond words, broke out:

"Marjory, even in jest, you shouldn't speak so. See, you have so horribly grieved your sister and uncle that they have gone away. You are loved very dearly; I think there is not one here who has not felt your words pierce them like a knife, and don't seek to inflict such terrible pain on others who are only hoping and anxious for your recovery. There, child, I didn't mean to speak harshly to you, but I cannot bear, none of us can, to hear you referring thus to the possibility of your not getting well again. Isn't it so, Miss Templeton, that she is mending? She would soon be well if she gave herself fair play, and laughed and talked less, would she not?" he urged, eagerly.

"Nothing can be healthier than laughter, and nothing sweeter than Marjory's," said Hamilton, in gloomy defence, as he looked

---

99. A play on Hamlet's famous lines uttered while holding the skull of the former court jester: 'Alas poor Yorick ...' in Shakespeare's *Hamlet*, 1601.

at Denzil. "Nevertheless, it is just as well we should leave this little witch with her witch-like delight in horrifying us; she must want rest now. Good-by, child."

He was not naturally demonstrative, but as he held the pale, soft, little hand in his, all the brightness she had made of this city house, the sunshine of her trials and aimless flatterings, her quaint poises midway between rest and energy, her indolent whims and graces and sweet nonsense rushed upon him like days of remembered gladness that can be no more. In that moment it seemed cruel that such an innocent, harmless flower should be cut down, and he, a man, with all a man's errors and ambitions, standing there beside her, full and strong and active. She could not harm anyone, and he, if he wished it, could; her life might have been sunshine and laughter because of mere existence, and there she lay like a crushed snowdrop, with that witchery and evanescent beauty fading from life.

No one cared to remain once Hamilton had given them the opportunity of leaving. It was too pitiful, too hopeless, too heart-rending. There was something solemn in each leave-taking, and when Morna returned after they had gone she found Marjory a mere atom of shuddering, pallid existence stilled fitfully into rigidity. The doctor came and shook his head—that was his verdict. No need of prescriptions or orders. When Marjory awoke to consciousness she felt for Morna's hand, which held her clasped in close embrace.

"Bring me his letters—they are upstairs with his likeness and books," she whispered. "I want to burn them now; I tried to do so before, but I couldn't. I must now."

Morna held the thin, white hand extended to the candle, and patiently, silently watched each letter crumble into ashes. The likeness was hard to burn, and Marjory gasped and shivered as she held it.

"Morna, you won't blame me now because I loved him so horribly. If I could have lived for you, for you—the very best in all the world—I would; but it was so lonely, so hard without Frank. You would have loved me more, I know, but I couldn't help loving him best. I tried not to, I did, dearest—oh, my very, very best and dearest; and you'll not blame me now that I failed and only realised how much better it would have been for me if I had never loved anyone but you. Won't you forgive me?"

"My darling," whispered Morna, hiding her terrible anguish in the waves of hair on her shoulder.

"You'll marry Denzil Dalrymple, and if you have a little girl you'll call her Marjory—won't you?" she gasped, breathlessly.

"There'll never be but the one Marjory for me. If she leaves me, all light and love and happiness will leave my life, too."

But Marjory scarcely heard the words; she was drifting fast into the sleep from which there is no awakening.

For Morna that week of mourning and desolation was terrible and as nearly reached despair as possible with a nature so deeply religious. One thing alone awoke her momently from her stupid rigid gaze on Marjory's dead face, and that was when her eyes, straying vaguely over all the details of the drapery and flowers which Miss Templeton and her friends had partly arranged, and with exquisite taste, she saw that everyone but herself had moved away from the bed and were staring in eager, angry curiosity at a man who had entered and was standing near her. She looked up and recognised Harston looking at his lost dead love in evident remorse and sorrow. He was just then thinking in bitterness of the gold he had exchanged for that bright gold hair curling round the poor, still little face, with its closed eyes and pale, mute lips. Morna drew herself in with a gasping, contracted shiver, and gazed on him in fascinated, strained horror. Before she could say a word he recognised his position, and, gently lifting a white narcissus which had rested near her hair, he kissed it, and went out.

But after the funeral Morna's numbed energies actively returned. She wrote at once to a convent in Harold's-cross on which her mind had been once before indefinitely fixed, and within a week all preparations had been made. The morning of her departure she visited Glasnevin in a last farewell of Marjory. Denzil had called each day, but had been refused admittance. On the bleak November day—the anniversary of the Manchester Martyrs—he learnt of her sad purpose and resolved to follow her to the cemetery.[100] He walked along and remembered Marjory's last chill reference to the place. Even then, through all his heavy sorrow he could not help smiling at the child's grotesque and persistent humour. She motioned him to follow the men who had come to celebrate the Anniversary, and Denzil had no idea how solemn and impressive such a small silent gathering of earnest men could be. Their simple prayers touched him intensely; their solemn "God save Ireland!" and bare heads filled with impersonal enthusiasm and he turned to leave with Morna even graver and paler than before.

"Is this farewell, Morna?"

"Yes. I am going because it is the best, the only life for me now. If it were otherwise I would gladly alter it, but don't seek to urge me to change now; you will only hurt me cruelly and make it worse for me," she added, beseechingly.

"I must regard your wish as a sacred command. I have nothing to say to you now except that I have loved you and will ever love you as the best, the sweetest, the holiest half of my soul. If ever I have to choose between good and evil, I have but to remember you, and good will be my choice. I will not say that I shall never marry, because one does not know, but if ever I do, and God

---

100. Manchester Martyrs: 'an attempt was made to rescue Fenian leaders Thomas Kelly and Timothy Deasy from police custody in Manchester. During the attempt, Police Sergeant Charles Brett was killed, causing strong anti-Irish feeling. Three Fenians, William Allen, Michael Larkin, and Michael O'Brien, were executed for the murder on 23 November. There was widespread indignation in Ireland and the 'martyrs', as they became known, were given a public funeral attended by over 60,000 people'. Cannon, John, and Robert Crowcroft. "Manchester martyrs". In *A Dictionary of British History*. Oxford University Press, https://www.oxfordreference.com/view/10.1093/acref/9780191758027.001.0001/acref-9780191758027-e-2227.

blesses me with a daughter, she shall be called Morna, and it will be my most sacred right to teach her to resemble you."

Nothing was said till they reached Leeson-street. Denzil followed her inside to say good-bye.

"Morna," he cried, "think of my obedience, when my life's best happiness is at stake, and say if I do not deserve one kiss to take with me into the long future as the past's best memory."

A delicate flush reached from throat to brow, and her eyes deepened in colour and lustre as she yielded him both hands and approached her face to his. One long look of love, a solemn kiss was their farewell. Four hours later the convent door had closed on Morna, and Denzil had applied for active service.

[THE END.]

THE GIRL'S REALM
February 1899: Vol. 1 No. 4

'A Girl Revolutionist'
BY HANNAH LYNCH

Moya O'Connell was seventeen when she left school, and read in solitude Mitchel's "History of Ireland".[1] She was not of an age to reason, and discover that things in Ireland have slightly changed since the lamentable days of Elizabeth or Cromwell, and that it requires something greatly other than mere stage oratory and flamboyant journalism to work a revolution in Ireland or elsewhere.

She studied the literature of '48 for two years, and then the crisis came.[2] Moya was a slim creature, very fair and vapoury, with large blue eyes that rarely saw anything, and looked at nothing. She lived in the clouds, recited Mangan's thrilling poem, "Dark Rosaleen," with striving, passionate gaze, and dreamed of freeing Ireland.[3]

These were exciting times. Men she took to be haloed heroes

---

1. John Mitchel (1815–1875), *History of Ireland Since the Treaty of Limerick* (Glasgow, London, and Dublin: Duffy 1868). Mitchel was an Irish nationalist and journalist whose complex and controversial life included revolutionary activities resulted in arrest, trial and transportation for treason in 1848. For further biographical details see John Quinn, John Mitchel, *DIB*. https://www.dib.ie/biography/mitchel-john-a5834
2. Literature of '48: a reference to the rebellion of 1848 by members of the Young Ireland Movement including William Smith O'Brien (1803–64) and John Mitchel (1815–1875).
3. James Clarence Mangan (1803–1849): Irish poet, translator, nationalist. "Dark Rosaleen" (1846), one of Mangan's most famous poems and translations, is both a love lament and political allegory. The eponymous Rosaleen personifies Ireland and national suffering. See Sean Ryder, *James Clarence Mangan, DIB*, https://www.dib.ie/biography/mangan-james-clarence-a5431

spent their free days making harrowing and eloquent speeches, and the intervals in writing a gorgeous revolutionary literature, in which Ireland literally waded knee-deep in Saxon blood, when they were not exposing the unimaginable horrors, noble and chivalrous young men were suffering in British dungeons. When they became too eloquent and too dangerous, they were speedily locked up in jail, and all the country went into mourning. It was a very serious and a very enthralling hour for Moya. She took the revolutionary fever with a gravity and intensity that might have cost her her life—at least, her reason.

Moya's uncle was a Conservative gentleman, who liked his book and his glass, and was on the best of terms with his landlord, Viscount Fitzelling. He owned a pretty little place, in a midland county, on the edge of a dull town. Moya, extremely frail and overwrought, was supposed to be resting excited nerves and tranquilising a disturbed pulse amid country sights and sounds, and silences; but this was to count without Moya's passionate patriotism and nervous system. Women all over Ireland had joined the fray, and marched in battalions to meet and defy the enemy.[4] The uncle, as I have said, was a man who loved his ease, and had a pleasant sense of humour. He mildly ridiculed his niece, and laughed at revolutionary Ireland. He did not believe in revolutions, but he knew better than to thwart the intense and inflammable Moya. She might revolutionise to her liking, and much good might it do her. Meanwhile England was there, Ireland was here, and the sea was between them. The advantage, he sarcastically hinted, was England's. In England's place, he owned, he would prefer the sea a little wider, that is all.

While meditating along the silent country roads, and beneath the stars at dusk, on the great things she would like to do, a couple of heroes of the nation came to spread the light in the neighbourhood. She went unnoticed to drink at the fount of eloquence. Beside her

---

4. Clearly a reference to the Ladies' Land League. Significantly, the militant language anticipates similar rhetoric typical of suffragette discourse in the early twentieth century.

at the meeting sat a spruce young farmer, in velveteen breeches and long boots. He addressed her by her name in a tone of deferential admiration, and, the meeting over, begged permission to accompany her to her uncle's, as the autumn evening was beginning to fall. She accepted, charmed to unburden her harassed soul to a fellow patriot. What could a gifted girl do to assist the cause of her downtrodden land? The young farmer had his answer pat. Found a league of patriotic young women in the nearest village. He would act as her knight, her secretary, and modestly rejoice in her glory.

Thus began the enchanting hours of conspiracy. They met by moonlight beyond the town bridge, and the murmuring river sang its silver song above their patriotic undertones. One evening Moya, after dinner, crept from her uncle's gate to the tryst, where a car and horse awaited her. The faithful secretary and she drove to the village, where a collection of patriotic women of all ages was gathered to hear from her young and ardent lips the words of wisdom, and constitute themselves, under her enlightenment, into a revolutionary body. It would be difficult to find a creature more inexperienced in all things than Moya O'Connell, but she believed in herself and in her mission, and this alone enabled Joan of Arc to work miracles.[5] As they sat deliberating on the quickest method of laying the British Empire in ruins, the secretary rushed into the hall of conference with the ghastly cry: "The police! The police."

In a twinkling an inspector and two constabulary men made their appearance, and the inspector bluntly exclaimed:

"Ladies, you must disperse."[6]

Moya stood up, and in her grandest manner, that she was the

---

5. See the reference to "Irish Joans of Arc" and note 86, p. 147 in this volume. Joan of Arc was also presented as a heroine elsewhere in the *Girl's Realm* (see Rodgers 2012).
6. A direct reference to Ladies' Land League meetings dispersed by the Royal Irish Constabulary, captured in an illustration for the *London Illustrated News* 24 December 1881 (see front cover) by Aloysius O'Kelly. Niamh O'Sullivan, 'Aloysius C. O'Kelly', *DIB*, https://www.dib.ie/biography/okelly-aloysius-c-a6828

President of the meeting, and protested against the presence of the police. The inspector regretted his duty, but he must take her name and address. Thanks to her uncle's influence, the incident had no desperate sequel. Moya would have preferred to stand like Robert Emmet[7] in the dock, and exhort her countrymen not to write her epitaph until Ireland should be free. She went home out-mannered, but not subdued.

Since the British Empire could not for a nod be overthrown, it was advisable to bring a nearer tyrant to his knees, and she and the secretary decided that the tenants should be eloquently instructed to pay Lord Fitzelling no rent until he showed himself in that abject position. Now the thing was to gather all the tenants spread over several acres of land together, and force them to come to a common accord. With this intent Moya sat up all night, with several quires of paper and packages of envelopes, on which she wrote out an imperative circular, inviting the tenants of Viscount Fitzelling to meet her, in their own interest, at a big barn chosen by the secretary, outside the town, at nine o'clock P.M. Those posted, the secretary and she, when the moon had dipped and the town lay folded in the mantle of night, stole out—she jumping from the low window of her chamber, and softly unhinging the gate, he carrying the paste-pot, brush, and sheaves of manifestoes newly printed in Dublin—and both affixed these illegal documents to every edifice along the street walls. The consternation of the Conservative uncle may be imagined when he found these manifestoes numerously spread along his private walls—he, the boonfellow and dearest friend of Viscount Fitzelling! He ordered his gardener to tear them down, but wisely forebore to connect the miscreant deed with the revolutionary disposition of his niece.

On the fatal day, Moya was silent at dinner, in the throes of mental oratory. The uncle was extremely facetious, and made merry over the picture of Paddy of Cork, furnished with a stick,

---

7. Robert Emmet (1788–1803): Irish nationalist, patriot and revolutionary. See p. 76, note 41 in this volume.

preparing to attack the British bayonets.[8] But Moya heeded him not. She was composing her famous address to the men of Ireland. At eight o'clock she stole upstairs, robed herself in her austerest raiment, but, preoccupied as she was, quite forgot to pin up her long fair plait. "Never mind," she said to herself, "I look like a French chevalier." She crept downstairs and through the hall door, and went rapidly down the dim avenue. The air was fragrant with moist autumn scents; the street beyond was empty. All the windows were blinded as she hurried along, and only now and then did she meet an indistinct form, that greeted her with a ringing "Good-night." Near the bridge she detected the clear profile through the dense shadow, of a car and a horse. "Is that you, Miss O'Connell?" softly breathed the secretary's voice.

She sprang upon the car, holding his hand, and they drove briskly over the bridge, hardly daring to exchange speech until they saw the outlines of the town huddled against the fluid obscurity of the backward heaven. The barn lay far onward, off the high road, with a high hedge of bramble and briar. A boy was found to hold the horse, and the two conspirators, in silence, crossed the slip of arch of the dim sky, a line of male forms showed in fantastic shadows. Moya's appearance was hailed with a patriotic cheer.

There are two things the Irish peasant profoundly respects and admires; womanhood and eloquence. Moya came to talk to them, and Moya was a pretty young woman. It needed no more to provoke enthusiasm. There were between sixty and eighty men, young and old. They wore corduroy, and twisted their felt caps in their hands. The police, thank God, were several miles away at the police station, and not a soul but themselves knew of the gathering.

Standing in their midst, after a cordial "Good evening, friends,"

---

8. Lynch addresses the negative stereotyping of Ireland and particularly the Ladies' Land League in press reports and satirical cartoons elsewhere, including 'Marjory Maurice'. Such satires appeared in magazine publications including *Punch*. See Binckes and Laing 2019, pp. 50–52.

Moya looked too slim and slight a figure to address from the ground these rough, obsequious giants. So the secretary brought a barrel, and stood it at the top of the big barn, and, assisted by him, Moya gravely took her place upon this platform. She cleared her throat, and in solemn, weighted tones began her magnificent address: "Men of Ireland." She, like the men around her, needed nothing but a few grandiloquent words to project her out of reality, and land her in a dream or a fairy tale.

The men of Ireland, packed in a big group in front of her, listened in open-mouthed, wide-eyed admiration. Words flowed from her on a hurrying wave, a mere magnificent void as far as sense went, but full of the seizing beauty that youth and passion alone can give the inane. She had convinced everyone present, from hoary age to beardless boyhood, that the sole means of rescuing Ireland from the grasp of the brutal Saxon lay in defrauding an insignificant nobleman of his rents. It's the fatal logic of mob eloquence all the world over. She, innocent child, believed every word she uttered. In your fresh and fervid teens—such reasoning may be condoned, since the history of the nineteenth century furnished us, in every land, with the spectacle of bearded men preaching this iniquitous inanity of doctrine. As if justice can ever spring from injustice! But in those wild days Ireland had gone off its head, and the sacred cause of freedom was supposed to repose upon the denial of human responsibilities. In the interests of "Dark Rosaleen," fathers of families, suffering mothers and hungry children were asked to commit themselves to the laneways, with the stars for their lamps, the sky for their tent, and mother earth for their couch. These sixty or eighty tenants of Viscount Fitzelling, not by any means a model landlord, but no wickeder than the rest of us who are not "model" in any path, had nearly pledged themselves to a man to pay no rent, but let themselves be brutally evicted to the last man of them for the non-fulfilment of accepted engagements, when there was a sound of hoofs along the dry road outside. "The police!" shouted the secretary in dismay.

All the revolutionists ranked themselves, ready to charge in battle array. To the last drop of their blood were they gallantly prepared to defend their maid. Woe betide the constabulary hand that should seek to touch her sacred shoulder!

"Have no fear," shouted an aged tenant. "We'll defend ye to the death, Miss," and a youth with flaming eyes added: "And depend upon it, Miss, divil a farthing will that blackguard Fitzelling get from any of us."

Moya stood gloriously upon her barrel, one hand firmly clutching the collar of her winter coat, the other extended in a noble oratorical gesture: "Men of Ireland," she exhorted.

The barn-door flew open, and her uncle, muffled, with felt hat over his eyes, stood upon the threshold. He gazed placidly round upon the mystified audience, glanced smilingly at his niece, who was staring with all her might at him, unfolded his heavy cloak, and ejaculated: "Pouf! what are you doing here, my friends? Don't you know right well what's the matter with her?" He touched his forehead significantly. "Poor girl! Mother's heartbroken. No harm in her at all, but——." Here he touched his forehead again.

Moya's eyes blazed ominously; to show anger was but to invite her own undoing, since it lent justification to her uncle's infamous insinuation. She gazed wildly round her, but the eyes of the men of Ireland were lowered. Their gallant intention to defend her to the death had changed to a meaner desire. They shuffled their feet and twisted their caubeens[9] in a disillusioned way. The Joan of Arc a moment ago now was nothing more than "a quare young woman" whom kindly relatives allowed at large. Upon a single impulse, in silence, the men of Ireland sloped.

Left alone with her uncle, unsupported even by the secretary in velveteen breeches and long boots, Moya scrambled down from her perch, and sat disconsolately on the barrel. She wanted to die at that moment. Her uncle came up the barn on the airiest tread.

---

9. Caubeen: Irish beret or a cap.

"Well, my dear, you see the value of your army. Heroes, every man-jack of them. Tomorrow you'll find every skulking house has slyly visited the agent, and paid his rent unbeknownst."

Her uncle was in the right of it. Every man by noon the next day, which was proper on their part, had paid his rent to Viscount Fitzelling; it temporarily broke Moya's heart. She regarded it as the basest of deceptions, regarded the monsters in corduroys as traitors to the cause, and imagined the freedom of Ireland retarded by at least a century by their scandalous disaffection. Yet, what could she do? She could not possibly assure them that she was not mad, or had never been sent to her uncle's for any brain trouble. Luckily the very morning after her silent and depressed drive back from the historic barn with her cynical and amused uncle, who enjoyed a merry hour with Lord Fitzelling, afterwards recounting to him the tale of Moya's prowess, eloquence, and discomfiture, she received a telegram, asking her to come up to Dublin, and replace the last editor of *Erin,* brutally carried off to the Government's dungeon cell that day.[10] She travelled up that same evening, and Lord Fitzelling was on the platform to see her off.

"By Jove!" exclaimed his lordship to her uncle, "a nice little devil, all the same. If she had stayed longer, I should have been in love with her."

In revolution there is no such thing as apprenticeship. There is something to be done, and the first person handy must do it, ill or well. A female editor of *Erin* was needed, and Moya's apparent duty, though she had never written a line for print, was to seize this occasion. Undaunted, she sat herself in the editor's chair, always forgetting to turn up that betraying blond pig-tail. Undeterred by the thought of prison or the gallows, she complacently killed off the Saxon in leaders, seemingly written in Saxon blood.

---

10. A thinly disguised reference to the proscription of *United Ireland* and the imprisonment of the editor, William O'Brien, in Kilmainham jail in 1881. The Ladies' Land League then took over the running and distribution of the paper.

Not capable of injuring a fly, she wrote with a pen fashioned of dynamite, and wiped out the British Institutions.

Never was *Erin* so virulent, so venomous, so spirited an organ. Mere males, when they wrote, had an eye upon the police, the castle, jail—maybe even the gallows. But Moya scorned all these considerations. The Lord Lieutenant was less to her than the office-boy; the gallows was merely as expeditive and heroic excursion into the next world; prison, a kind of national picnic. In her office leisure she composed a philosophic novel, containing her exceedingly mature views of life and hereafter, and at half-past seven she dined at a quiet restaurant in the vicinity, with other lady revolutionists.

It was, I have said, an exciting time. Everybody in the delectable city, and even overseas, went "shadowed," and not to be in prison was to be a nobody. The prisoners themselves had fine times. Ladies formed committees to supply them with the latest delicacies and luxuries; men who had fed upon the coarser diet hitherto, now ate salmon and strawberries, game, delicate viands of every sort, and ices. Labouring men, heroically suffering confinement in an agreeable national institution, made bitter complaints if the breakfast sole was not fresh, though sole were a delicacy they had hitherto never tasted.[11]

The eyes of the Government were upon Moya, and the fiery organ she so fierily edited was doomed. One evening, as she returned from dining at the quiet restaurant mentioned, she saw a line of detectives drawn up outside the office. She slipped through the band, until the chief arrested her march.

"Who are you, Miss?" he asked blandly.

"I'm the acting editor," she said, with her grandest revolutionary air.

The chief detective, not believing her, and amused by her

---

11. Numerous first hand and later accounts of the Kilmainham prison experience for members of the Land League corroborate Lynch's description here. See for example, Tighe Hopkins 1896, p. 16.

juvenile audacity, let her pass. Crowds of men and women were gathered inside in a state of dismayed excitement. The paper was all ready to appear next day, and the order had come from the Castle to seize it. The eight stereo plates were ready for print, and somebody cried, "Oh, if it could only be got to London, it could appear by Saturday."[12]

"Get a cab round by the back entrance," cried Moya, "and have the plates carried into it. I'll go across to England with them tonight."

The resolution was hailed with general delight, and while the detectives, step by step, were making their way in, the printers were carrying, to a cab behind, the sacred plates of *Erin*.

Then came the midnight helter-skelter drive across the city, the snatched sleep at a seaside hotel, the wakening with the dawn, the hasty meal of coffee and bacon, and rush down to the boat, while the moon was yet in the wavering heavens, and then by sunrise Ireland was just a bright blot against the mounting blue. Then grey waves, and the cold salt air blowing, and always that yellow iron box with its awful contents sitting upon her imagination. It had not been weighed or examined, thanks to a couple of obliging sailors. But how would it be at the other side, on the enemy's fatal shores?

At Holyhead,[13] with a frozen sensation gripping her heartstrings, Moya recognised a posse of detectives. Nobody, of course, noticed her, but all eyes she saw were upon the terrible yellow iron box. It stood on the middle of the platform, an object of visible suspicion. Station-master, porters, detectives, stood around it, evidently in expectation of a dynamite explosion. Nobody could lift it, and it bore a woman's name, Miss Emily Fitzgibbon.

12. The events that follow are autobiographical. Katharine Tynan (1924, p. 163) and Henry George (Wenzer, ed. 2009, p. 52) both allude to Lynch's involvement in smuggling out stereo-plates and enabling the continued publication of *United Ireland*. This short story appears to be Lynch's only specific reference to her involvement.
13. Holyhead: a port on Holy Island in Wales and regularly used in crossings between Ireland and Britain.

'A GIRL REVOLUTIONIST'

Now Moya had clean forgotten her name, and sat back in a second-class carriage, striving to look as if she never possessed such a thing as a trunk in her life. The station-master kept back the train, and slowly went from carriage to carriage, asking for Miss Emily Fitzgibbon.

The porters were locking the doors, the station-master was on the point of lifting his whistle, when Moya in despair, struggled with the door of her carriage, and succeeded in flinging herself out upon the platform. She knocked up against a passenger as excited as she, and running to catch his seat at the last moment.

"Oh, Lord Fitzelling," she blurted out, recognising her uncle's friend, and one of the enemies of Ireland. "My box! I can't go without it. It's of the utmost moment."

Lord Fitzelling uncovered, followed her anguished gaze, and nodded to the station-master. "Here's my card," he cried; "this young lady is a friend of mine. Have the thing shoved into the van; it's my affair!"

"Are you Miss Emily Fitzgibbon?" sternly asked the station-master of Moya.

"No!" stammered Moya.

"It's a box Miss O'Connell is in charge of for a friend! Hurry now, don't let us lose the train," cried the peer, jovially, and followed Moya to her second-class carriage.

"I'll see you through this affair, whatever it is, Miss O'Connell, for you're a little brick;[14] but I say, you know, it's too bad if you're bringing over a box of no-rent manifestos and pots of paste to England to demoralise the tenantry of innocent landlords."

"Oh no, it's—"

---

14. A phrase originating in the Victorian period and recurring in popular fiction and conversation ascribing courage and integrity to a character. Nakul Krishna, '"You're a brick": colloquialism and the history of moral concepts'. *History of European Ideas,* 2019, vol. 45, no.3, pp. 410–420; See also Mary Cadogan and Patricia Craig. *You're a Brick, Angela!: A New Look at Girls' Fiction from 1839 to 1975.* London: Gollancz, 1976.

She stopped short, and Lord Fitzelling looked at her quizzically and smiled.

"It's your first batch of illusions, child. Would you believe it, when I left Cambridge twenty years ago I dreamed of freeing Ireland. We all go through it and recover."

Select Bibliography

Hannah Lynch's Girl Revolutionaries, New Girl and New Woman Fiction

___. 'A Girl Revolutionist'. *The Girl's Realm*, vol. 1, February 1889.
___. 'A Girl's Ride on an Engine'. *The Girl's Realm*, vol. 2, March 1900.
___ (et al). 'Christmas on the Hills: Tales'. *The Shamrock*, Christmas Double Number, December 1883–January 1884.
___. *Daughters of Men: A Novel*. London: William Heinemann, 1892.
___. 'Defeated'. London: *Beeton's Christmas Annual*, 1885.
___. *Denys d'Auvrillac. A Story of French Life*. London: J. Macqueen, 1896.
___. *Dr Vermont's Fantasy and Other Stories*. London: J. M. Dent & Co., 1896.
___. *Jinny Blake: A Tale*. London: J. M. Dent & Co., 1897.
___. 'La Puda de Montserrat'. *The Shamrock*, 26 November–10 December 1881.
___. 'Marjory Maurice'. *The Shamrock*, 27 December 1884–28 March 1885.
___. *The Prince of the Glades*. 2 volumes, London: Methuen, 1891.
___. *Rosni Harvey, A Novel*. 3 volumes, London: Chapman & Hall, 1892.
___. *Through Troubled Waters*. London, New York: Ward, Lock & Co., 1885.

Other Primary Sources

Gibbs, John P. 'Tribute to Hannah Lynch: An Irishwoman of Great Literary Ability Who Did Hard Work in the Parnell Movement'. *Gaelic American* [February], 1904.
Grand, Sarah. 'The New Aspect of the Woman Question'. *North American Review*, vol. 158, no. 3, 1894, pp. 270–276.
Hopkins, Tighe. *Kilmainham Memories*. London: Ward, Lock and Bowden, 1896.
Parnell, Anna. 1986. *The Tale of a Great Sham*, edited by Dana Hearne, Dublin: University College Dublin Press, 2020.
Turpin, John. 'Exhibitions of Art and Industries in Victorian Ireland: Part II: Dublin Exhibitions of Art and Industries 1865–1885'. *Dublin Historical Record*, vol. 35, no. 2, 1982, pp. 42–51.
Tynan, Katharine. *Twenty-Five Years: Reminiscences*. London: Smith Elder, 1913.
___. *Memories*. London: Everly Nash and Grayson, 1924.

Studies of Late Nineteenth-Century Irish Women's Writing

Binckes, Faith and K. Laing. *Hannah Lynch 1859–1904: Irish writer, Cosmopolitan, New Woman*. Cork: Cork University Press, 2019.

Campbell, Matthew, editor. *Irish Literature in Transition 1830–1880*. Cambridge: Cambridge University Press, 2020.

Coleman, Ann. 'Far from Silent: Nineteenth-Century Irish Women Writers'. *Public and Private Spheres: Gender Perspectives in Nineteenth-Century Ireland*, edited by Margaret Kelleher and James H. Murphy, Dublin: Irish Academic Press, 1997, pp. 203–211.

D'hoker, Elke, Raphaël Ingelbien, and Hedwig Schwall, editors. *Irish Women Writers: New Critical Perspectives*. New York: Peter Lang, 2011.

Foster, John Wilson. *Irish Novels 1890–1940: New Bearings in Culture and Fiction*. Oxford: Oxford University Press, 2008.

Hansson, Heidi. *Emily Lawless 1845–1913: Writing the Interspace*. Cork: Cork University Press, 2007.

___, editor. New *Contexts: Re-Framing Nineteenth-Century Irish Women's Prose*. Cork: Cork University Press, 2008.

Ingman, Heather. *Irish Women's Fiction: From Edgeworth to Enright*. Dublin: Irish Academic Press, 2013.

___ and Cliona Ó Gallchoir, editors. *A History of Modern Irish Women's Literature*. Cambridge: Cambridge University Press, 2018.

Kelleher, Margaret. 'Writing Irish Women's Literary History'. *Irish Studies Review*, vol. 9, no.1, 2001, pp. 5–14.

___. 'Prose writing and drama in English 1830–1890: from Catholic emancipation to the fall of Parnell'. *The Cambridge History of Irish Literature*, vol. 1, edited by Margaret Kelleher and Philip O' Leary, Cambridge: Cambridge University Press, 2006, pp. 449–99.

___. *The Feminization of Famine: Expressions of the Inexpressible*. Cork: Cork University Press, 1997.

___ and James H. Murphy. *Gender Perspectives in Nineteenth-Century Ireland: Public and Private Spheres*. Dublin: Irish Academic Press, 1997.

Laing, Kathryn and Sinéad Mooney, editors. *Irish Women Writers at the Turn of the Twentieth Century: Alternative Histories, New Narratives*. Brighton: Edward Everett Root Publishers, 2020.

Murphy, James H. 'Fiction, 1845–1900'. *A History of Modern Irish Women's Literature*, edited by Heather Ingman & Clíona Ó Gallchoir. Cambridge: Cambridge University Press, 2018, pp. 96–113.

___. *Irish Novelists & the Victorian Age*. Oxford: Oxford University Press, 2011.

Pilz, Anna and Standlee, Whitney, editors. *Irish Women's Writing, 1878–1922*. Manchester: Manchester University Press, 2016.

Standlee, Whitney. *Power to Observe: Irish Women Novelists in Britain, 1890–1916*. Bern: Peter Lang, 2015.

The Ladies' Land League and Irish Land War Fiction

Binckes, Faith and Laing, Kathryn. '"Rival attractions of the season": Land War Fiction, Christmas Annuals, and the Early Writing of Hannah Lynch'. *Fictions of the Irish Land War*, edited by Heidi Hansson and James H. Murphy, Bern: Peter Lang, 2014, pp. 57–80.

Groves, Patricia. *Petticoat Rebellion: The Anna Parnell Story.* Cork: Mercier Press, 2009.

Hansson, Heidi, and James H. Murphy, editors. *Fictions of the Irish Land War*, Bern: Peter Lang, 2014.

Kelleher, Margaret. '"Factual Fictions": Representations of the Land Agitation in Nineteenth-Century Women's Fiction'. *New Contexts: Re-Framing Nineteenth-Century Irish Women's Prose*, edited by Heidi Hansson, Cork: Cork University Press, 2008, pp. 78–91.

Laird, Heather. 'Decentring the Irish Land War: Women, Politics and the Private Sphere'. *Land Questions in Modern Ireland*, edited by Fergus Campbell and Tony Varley, Manchester: Manchester University Press, 2013, pp. 175–193.

Lucey, Donnacha Seán. 'Power, Politics and Poor Relief during the Irish Land War, 1879–82'. *Irish Historical Studies*, vol. 37, no. 148, 2011, pp. 584–98.

McL. Côté, Jane. *Fanny and Anna Parnell. Ireland's Patriot Sisters.* New York: St. Martin's, 1991.

Mulligan, Adrian N. '"By a Thousand Ingenious Feminine Devices": The Ladies' Land League and the Development of Irish Nationalism'. *Historical Geography*, vol. 37, 2009, pp. 159–177.

Murphy, James. H. 'Frenzied Form: The Land War Novel' in *Irish Novelists and the Victorian Age*, Oxford: Oxford University Press, 2011.

O'Cinnéide, Muireann. 'Anne Blunt, "Arabi Pasha"' and the Irish Land Wars, 1880–8'. *Women Writing War: Ireland 1880–1922*, edited by Tina O'Toole, Gillian McIntosh and Muireann O'Cinnéide, Dublin: University College Dublin Press, 2016, pp. 25–38.

O'Neill, Marie. 'The Ladies' Land League'. *Dublin Historical Record*, vol. 35, no. 4, September 1982, pp. 122–133.

O'Sullivan, Niamh. *Every dark hour: a history of Kilmainham Jail.* Liberties, Dublin, 2007

___. *Aloysius O'Kelly: Art, Nation, Empire.* Dublin: Field Day Publications; Notre Dame: Notre Dame University Press, 2010.

___. 'The Iron Cage of Femininity: Visual Representation of Women in the 1880s Land Agitation'. *Ideology and Ireland in the Nineteenth Century*, edited by Tadhg Foley & Seán Ryder, Dublin: Four Courts Press, 1998, pp. 181–196.

Schneller, Beverley E. *Anna Parnell's Political Journalism.* Bethesda: Academica Press, 2005.

Travers, Pauric. '"No Turning Back": Anna Parnell, Identity, Memory and Gender'. *The Ivy Leaf: The Parnells Remembered*, edited by Donal McCarthy and Pauric Travers, Dublin: University College of Dublin Press, 2006, pp. 124–139.

Urquhart Diane. '"The Ladies' Land League have [sic] a crust to share with you":

the Rhetoric of the Ladies' Land League's British Campaign, 1881–1882'. *Women Writing War: Ireland 1880–1922,* edited by Tina O'Toole, Gillian McIntosh and Muireann O'Cinnéide, Dublin: University College Dublin Press, 2016, pp. 11–24.

Ward, Margaret. 'Anna Parnell: Challenges to Male Authority and the Telling of National Myth'. *Parnell Reconsidered,* edited by Pauric Travers and Donal McCarthy, Dublin: University College Press, 2013, pp. 47–60.

___. 'A Terrible Beauty? Women, Modernity and Irish Nationalism before the Easter Rising'. *Knowing Their Place: The Intellectual Life of Women in the 19th Century,* edited by Brendan Walsh, Dublin: History Press, 2015, pp. 66–84.

___. *Unmanageable Revolutionaries: Women and Nationalism.* London: Pluto Press, 1995.

___. 'Gendering the Union: Imperial Feminism and the Ladies' Land League'. *Women's History Review,* vol. 10, no.1, 2001, pp. 71–92.

___. 'The Ladies' Land League and the Irish Land War 1881/2: Defining the Relationship between Women and Nation'. *Gendered Nations: Nationalisms and Gender Order in the Long Nineteenth Century,* edited by Ida Blom, Karen Hagemann and Catherine Hall, New York: Berg Publishers, 2000, pp. 229–247.

Wenzer, Kenneth C., editor. *Henry George, the Transatlantic Irish, and Their Times.* Bingley: Emerald Group Publishing, 2009.

Newspaper, Periodical and Print Cultures

Andrews, Ann. *Newspapers and Newsmakers: The Dublin Nationalist Press in the Mid-Nineteenth Century.* Liverpool: Liverpool University Press, 2014.

Dungan, Myles. *Mr Parnell's Rottweiler: Censorship and the United Ireland Newspaper, 1881–1891.* Dublin: Irish Academic Press, 2014.

Easley, Alexis, Clare Gill, and Beth Rodgers, editors *Women, Periodicals and Print Culture in Britain, 1830s-1900s: The Victorian Period.* Edinburgh: Edinburgh University Press, 2019.

Hayley, Barbara. '"A Reading and Thinking Nation": Periodicals as the Voice of Nineteenth Century Ireland'. *Three Hundred Years of Irish Periodicals,* edited by Barbara Hayley and Enda McKay, Mullingar: Association of Irish Learned Journals, 1987, pp. 29–48.

Legg, Marie-Louise. *Newspapers and Nationalism: The Irish Provincial Press, 1850–1892.* Dublin: Four Courts Press, 1999.

Murphy, James H. 'Novelists, Publishers and Readers, 1830–90'. *The Oxford History of the Irish Book in English 1800–1891,* edited by James Murphy, Oxford: Oxford University Press, 2011, pp. 411–19.

___. '"Things Which Seem to You Unfeminine": Gender and Nationalism in the Fiction of Some Upper Middle-Class Catholic Women Novelists, 1880–1910'. *Border Crossings: Irish Women Writers and National Identities,* edited by Kathryn Kirkpatrick, Tuscaloosa: University of Alabama Press, 2000, pp. 58–78.

Nic Congáil, Ríona. '"Fiction, Amusement, Instruction": The Irish Fireside Club and the Educational Ideology of the Gaelic League'. *Eire-Ireland,* vol. 44, nos. 1&2,

Spring and Summer 2009, pp. 91–117.

___. 'Young Ireland and the Nation: Nationalist Children's Culture in the Late Nineteenth Century'. *Eire-Ireland*, vol. 46, nos. 3&4, Winter 2011, pp. 37–68.

North, John S. *The Waterloo Directory of Irish Newspapers and Periodicals, 1800–1900*. Waterloo Ont.: North Waterloo Academic Press, 1986.

Rains, Stephanie. '"Nauseous Tides of Seductive Debauchery": Irish Story Papers and the Anti-Vice Campaigns of the Early Twentieth Century'. *Irish University Review*, vol. 45, 2015, pp. 263–280.

___. 'Thrilling Tales and Shocking Stories – Story Papers in Ireland'. *Irish Media History* blog, October 22, 2015, https://irishmediahistory.com/category/story-papers/

___. 'Popular Prints'. *Irish Literature in Transition, 1830–1880*, edited by Matthew Campbell, vol. 3, Cambridge University Press, Cambridge, 2020, pp. 299–317.

Tilley, Elizabeth. *The Periodical Press in Nineteenth-Century Ireland*. London: Palgrave, 2020.

Periodical Fiction, the (Irish) New Girl and the (Irish) New Woman

Bilston, Sarah. *The Awkward Age in Women's Popular Fiction, 1850–1900: Girls and the Transition to Womanhood*. Oxford: Clarendon Press, 2004.

Binckes, Faith and Kathryn Laing. 'From "Wild Irish Girl" to "Parisianised Foreigner": Hannah Lynch and France'. *War of the Words: Literary Rebellion in France and Ireland*, edited by Eamon Maher and Eugene O'Brien, Rennes: Publication du CRBC Rennes-2, TIR, 2010, pp. 41–58.

___. 'A Vagabond's Scrutiny: Hannah Lynch in Europe'. *Irish Women Writers: New Critical Perspectives*, edited by Elke D'Hoker, Raphaël Ingelbien, and Hedwig Schwall, Bern: Peter Lang, 2011, pp. 111–131.

Bittel, Helen. 'Required Reading for "Revolting Daughters"?: The New Girl Fiction of L.T. Meade'. *Nineteenth-Century Gender Studies*, vol. 2, no. 2, Summer 2006. http://www.ncgsjournal.com/issue22/bittel.html

Cahill, Susan. 'Making Spaces for the Irish Girl: Rosa Mulholland and Irish Girls in Fiction at the Turn of the Century'. *Colonial Girlhood in Literature, Culture and History, 1840–1950*, edited by Kristine Moruzi and Michelle Smith, London: Palgrave Macmillan, 2014, pp. 167–179.

___. 'Where are the Irish Girls? Girlhood, Irishness, and LT Meade'. *Girlhood and the Politics of Place*, edited by Claudia Mitchell and Carrie Rentschler, New York: Berghahan Books, 2016, pp. 212–227.

Dawson, Janis. 'The Politics of Naughtiness in L. T. Meade's School Fiction'. *English Literature in Transition, 1880–1920*, vol. 63, no. 3, 2020, pp. 400–428.

Edwards, Heather. 'The Irish New Woman and Emily Lawless's *Grania: The Story of an Island*: A Congenial Geography'. *English Literature in Transition*, 1880–1920, vol. 51.4, 2008, pp. 421–438.

Gray, Alexandra. *Self-Harm in New Woman Writing*. Edinburgh University Press, Edinburgh, 2019.

Heilmann, Ann. *The Late-Victorian Marriage Question: A Collection of Key New Woman Texts*. vol. 4, Abingdon: Taylor & Francis, 1998.
Ledger, Sally. *The New Woman: Fiction and Feminism at the Fin de Siècle*. Manchester: Manchester University Press, 1997.
Mangum, Teresa. *Married, Middlebrow and Militant: Sarah Grand and the New Woman Novel*. Ann Arbor: University of Michigan Press, 1998.
Mitchell, Sally. *The New Girl: Girls' Culture in England, 1880–1915*. New York: Columbia University Press, 1995.
Moruzi, Kristine. *Constructing Girlhood Through the Periodical Press, 1850–1915*. Aldershot: Ashgate, 2012.
___ and Michelle J. Smith, editors. *Colonial Girlhood in Literature, Culture and History, 1840–1950*. London: Palgrave Macmillan, 2014.
O'Toole, Tina. 'Ireland: The *Terra Incognita* of the New Woman Project'. *New Contexts: Re-Framing Nineteenth-Century Irish Women's Prose*, edited by Heidi Hansson, Cork: Cork University Press, 2008, pp. 125–41.
___. *The Irish New Woman*. New York: Palgrave Macmillan, 2013.
___. 'The (Irish) New Woman: Political, Literary, and Sexual Experiments'. *The History of British Women's Writing, 1880–1920*, edited by Holly Laird, Basingstoke: Palgrave Macmillan, 2016, pp. 23–34.
___. 'New Irish Women and New Women's Writing'. *Irish Literature in Transition, 1880–1940*, edited by Marjory Howes, Cambridge: Cambridge University Press, 2020, pp. 152–170.
Rodgers, Beth. 'The Editor of the Period: Alice Corkran, the *Girl's Realm* and the Woman Editor'. *Women, Periodicals and Print Culture in Britain, 1830s–1900s: The Victorian Period*, by Alexis Easley, Clare Gill and Beth Rodgers, Edinburgh: Edinburgh University Press, 2019, pp. 164–177.
___. *Adolescent Girlhood and Literary Culture at the Fin De Siècle: Daughters of Today*. Basingstoke: Palgrave Macmillan, 2016.
___. 'Competing Girlhoods: Competition, Community, and Reader Contribution in the *Girl's Own Paper* and *The Girl's Realm*'. *Victorian Periodicals Review*, vol. 45, no.3, 2012, pp. 277–300.
___. 'Irishness, Professional Authorship, and the 'Wild Irish Girls' of L.T. Meade'. *English Literature in Transition 1880–1920*, vol. 56, no.2, 2013, pp. 146–166.
___. 'I am glad I am Irish through and through and through: Irish Girlhood and Identity in L.T. Meade's *Light O' the Morning; or, The Story of an Irish Girl* (1899)'. *Colonial Girlhood in Literature, Culture and History, 1840–1950*, edited by Kristine Moruzi and Michelle Smith, London: Palgrave Macmillan, 2014, pp. 154–166.
Roos, B. 'Unlikely Heroes: Katharine Tynan's *The Story of Bawn*, the Irish Famine, and the Sentimental Tradition'. *Irish University Review*, vol. 43, no. 2, 2013, pp. 327–343.
Sunderland, Helen. '"Politics for Girls": Representations of Political Girlhood in the *Girl's Own Paper* and the *Girl's Realm*'. *Victorian Periodicals Review*, vol. 52, no. 1, 2019, pp. 1–26.

Also published by *EER*
Available now...

Yeats Revisited
The Continuing Legacy

DAVID PIERCE

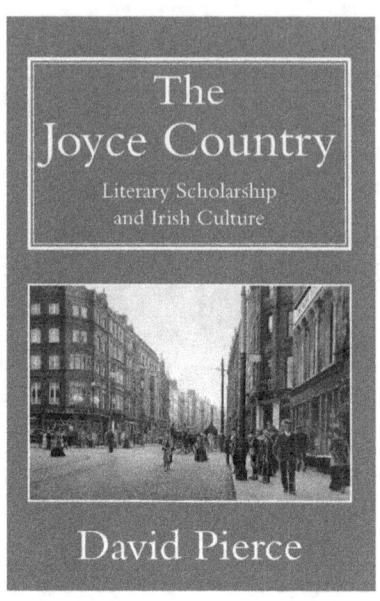

The Joyce Country
Literary Scholarship and Irish Culture

David Pierce

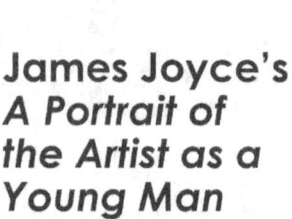

James Joyce's *A Portrait of the Artist as a Young Man*

David Pierce

THE NECESSARY FICTION
Life with James Joyce's Ulysses

Michael Groden

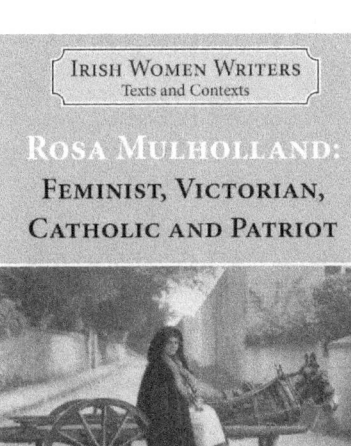

www.ingramcontent.com/pod-product-compliance
Lightning Source LLC
Chambersburg PA
CBHW062227300426
44115CB00012BA/2254